DESIGN BOOK EIGHT

ORIGINAL FURNITURE FROM THE WORLD'S FINEST CRAFTSMEN

DESIGN BOOK EIGHT

ORIGINAL FURNITURE FROM THE WORLD'S FINEST CRAFTSMEN

SCOTT GIBSON

The Taunton Press

The Taunton Press
Inspiration for hands-on living®

The Taunton Press, Inc., 63 South Main Street,
PO Box 5506, Newtown, CT 06470-5506
e-mail: tp@taunton.com

Editor: Anatole Burkin
Copy editor: Elizabeth Healy
Jacket/cover design: Don Morris Design
Interior design: Michael Amaditz
Interior layout: Michael Amaditz, Kat Riehle
Illustrator: Robert La Pointe

Library of Congress Cataloging-in-Publication Data
Gibson, Scott, 1951-
  Fine woodworking design book eight : original furniture from the world's finest craftsmen / Scott
Gibson.
      p. cm.
  Includes index.
  ISBN 978-1-60085-059-2
  1. Furniture--United States--History--21st century--Catalogs. I. Title.
  NK2408.2.G53 2009
  749--dc22
                                          2008042193

Printed in the United States of America
10 9 8 7 6 5 4 3 2 1

ACKNOWLEDGMENTS

Design Book Eight would not exist without the participation of a talented woodworking community, and we gratefully acknowledge the many furnituremakers who took the time to submit their work. In the end, we had more than we could squeeze into these pages. But in the coming months we hope to publish more of what we received in *Fine Woodworking* magazine's Reader Gallery and at www.finewoodworking.com. Special thanks to all of our participants:

Kimberly Winkle
Clark Kellogg
Duncan W. Gowdy
Mark Levin
Jon Siegel
Katie Hudnall
Jon Francis
Alexandra Geske
James Schriber
Jeff O'Brien
Don Green
Christopher Solar
Todd Ouwehand
David Hurwitz
Michael Singer
Peter Chen
John Thoe
Nick Boynton
Steve Holman
Roger Heitzman
Michael Gloor
Jeff Miller
Kevin P. Rodel
Seth Rolland
Scott M. King
Craig Thibodeau
John M. Godfrey II
S. Lloyd Natof
Curtis Erpelding
Todd Partridge
David Upfill-Brown
Pat Morrow
Ron Mascitelli
Brian Bortz
Curtis Minier
Matt Hutton
Loy Martin
Bill Huston
Susan Working
Seth A. Barrett
John Marckworth
Tyler Chartier
Peter S. Loh
Jim Postell
William Doub
Jennifer Anderson
Kevin Gill

Peter G. Thompson
Chris Bach
Greg Klassen
Hank Holzer
Paul Stefanski
Miguel Gomez-Ibanez
Eric Connor
Roy Alan Slamm
James Hoyne
Kay Selle
Greg Smith
Roger Savatteri
Aspy Khambatta
Rick Gorman
Bob Kopf
Tony Kenway
Timothy Coleman
Craig Jentz
Paulus Wanrooij
Alexandria Reznikoff
Thomas J. Monahan
Hugh N. Montgomery
Leah Woods
Celia Greiner
Mark Sfirri
David W. Hogan
Thomas R. Schrunk
Gary Rogowski
Nate Blaisdell
Katrina Tompkins
Ryan McNew
Aurelio Bolognesi
Curtis Buchanan
Ted Blachly
Jason Schneider
Michael Cullen
Brian M. Condran
Peter S. Turner
John Ransom Phillips
J-P Vilkman
John Grew Sheridan
Bob Passaro
Phil Watts
J. Harvey Baker
Mitch Roberson
Jeff Lind
Greg Moffatt

Vic Ptasznik
Peter Young
Chris Davidson
George Gaines III
Neil Lamens
Steve Butler
Les Thede
Ariel Kemp
Daryl Rosenblatt
Steve Szilvagyi
Edward Monteith
Michael Roske
Leigh Dean
Andrew Pitts
Dan Bollock
Kevin Basto
David Bley
Brian S. Fuller
Eugene DeSombre
Lubo Brezina
Ben Manns
Marie Kline
Ted Lott
Thomas C. Bennett
James Smith
Nevin Peters
Paul Mirocha
Jesse Bickel
Earl Osborne
Charlie Kolarik
Jesse Shaw
George W. Cook Jr.
David Blackburn
Ramon Valdez
Bert Johansen
Steve Skonieczny
David Bruce McCreary
Mark Laub
Glen G. Guarino
Phillip Tennant
Austin Rhodes
Rob Brown
Brad Warstler
Todd Graves
Michael Doran
Charlie Beier
Russell Garcia-Lechelt

Tim Siranberg
David L. Spray
Robert Porcaro
Mark Wedekind
Jeffrey R. Patrick
Julie Tsivia Cohen
Damon McIntyre
Tom Kiewitt
Aaron Fedarko
Tim Neun
Andy Maisel
Blaine Johnston
Terence Gerbrandt
James David Lee
S. Richard Jensen
Mary LuLehman
Jacque Allen
Michael Childs
Anthony Brozna
Frank DeJong
Joseph Murphy
Bob Rueter
R. Thomas Tedrowe, Jr.
Todd Crutchfield
Tony Mancini
Dan Clarke
Steven White
Andrew Glenn
Chantal Bonnant
Frederick Lipp
Barry Chattell
Robert C. Brand
Eugene Plawutsky
Derek Weidman
Kendall Lyons
Jeffrey Greene
Ivan Elvik
Melvin E. Simpson
James William Schuler III
Vaughn Tan
Margaret E. Polcawich
Anna C. Thornton
Aaron Russel
John Isch
Saer T. Huston
Thomas J. Smith
Brian McCambridge

Dale Johnson
Robert C.G. Hottentot
John Von Dis
Chris Nyklewicz
Aaron Levi
Derek Rund
Scott & Stephanie Shangraw
Terry Bachman
Bob Marsh
Dustin J. Farnsworth
Elizabeth Sweet
Philip Gaven
Elizabeth Phillips
Jerry Cousins
John W. Flanagan
Peter Tabur
Marcus Collier
Robin McKann
Tom Bader
Jared J. Boyd
David Linebarger
Alan Carter
Gerry Leistikow
Erick & Mitchel Osman
Jonathan Benso
Yoav S. Liberman
Rick Broemel
Ian Stewart
Ruud Joling
Mark Munson
Randall B. Griffin
Lance Klien
Norman Pirollo
Scott Smith
Gregory Ruppe
Michael Stadler
Mark Cwik
German Plessl
Mark Davis
Jason Wade
Jerry Spady
Fred Johnson
John Andrich
Judith Ames
Lee Hansen
Lee Erdman
Michael Powell

CONTENTS

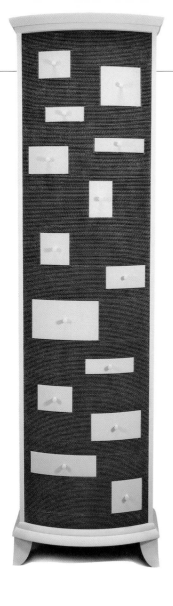

1

INTRODUCTION

It has been more than a dozen years since *Fine Woodworking* magazine published *Design Book Seven,* the most recent in a series that periodically explored contemporary woodworking. As was the case with its predecessors, this last iteration included a little bit of everything—not only chairs and desks and beds but also carvings and sculpture, even a hand-cranked wooden toy. It was a compilation of the best and most imaginative work that came to the attention of editors at *Fine Woodworking.*

In the interim, The Taunton Press launched and eventually folded *Home Furniture,* a magazine devoted to furniture design, not construction. Although *Home Furniture* never quite managed the circulation it needed for long-term survival, its demise left many woodworkers wishing there were more opportunities to look at current work. So, late last year, *Fine Woodworking* Publisher Anatole Burkin decided the time was right for an updated version of the *Design Book* series.

There would be several changes between the old series and its offspring, what first became F*ine Woodworking Furniture: 102 Contemporary Designs* published

last fall as a magazine, and now republished in book form as *Design Book Eight.*

For starters, *Design Book Eight* is limited to functional furniture, meaning that turnings, sculpture, musical instruments and the like would not be included. How come? We wanted to reach the greatest number of furnituremakers with design ideas that would be useful in their own work. We also decided to limit the collection to contemporary pieces. In making that early decision, we realized we would be excluding the many talented furnituremakers who turn out first-rate period reproductions. Yet we hoped it also would keep the collection more focused and more accessible.

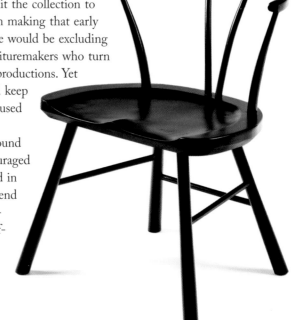

With those loose ground rules in place, we encouraged furnituremakers to send in their best work—and send they did. Once submissions were all in (a half-

dozen large cardboard boxes worth) they were re-viewed by a group of four: Anatole Burkin; Helen Albert, executive editor of Taunton books; and two former editors at *Fine Woodworking*, Jonathan Binzen, now a consulting editor, and me. All of us are wood-workers. Jessica DiDonato from the Taunton books staff provided the considerable editorial assistance the project required.

Readers with some of the early *Design Books* in their libraries may remember that each piece was accom-panied by a simple caption listing the basics: name of the maker, name of the piece (if it had one), materials, dimensions. We thought it would be interesting to include more this time so we sent questionnaires to each of the artisans who had been selected and asked them to tell us about themselves, their shops, how they worked and what they had in mind with the design of the piece or pieces we had selected. Their answers were variably rich with detail, painfully short or

something in between. But in any case, it was an opportunity for these artists and artisans to explain in their own words such things as how they arrived at a design, why they used a certain kind of wood and what their shops and work schedules are like. It has been an opportunity for us to peer into their creative train of thought. When you see a direct quote from a maker, that's where it comes from.

One thing that hasn't changed, though, is the quality of the work you'll find in these pages. As you'll see, there's still plenty of that.

—*Scott Gibson*

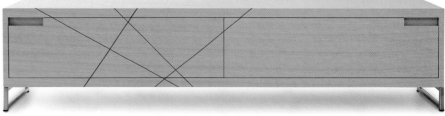

TABLES

Four legs and a top equal a table, and the Shakers proved that elemental doesn't have to be boring. Their spare designs were clean, elegant in their simplicity, and highly functional.

Some contemporary makers have continued to refine this minimalist approach by winnowing away unnecessary material in ever lighter frames. Traditional joinery can give way to nuts and bolts, or even copper rivets. Others have abandoned geometric regularity in their designs with asymmetrical bases and tops. Their tables become fluid and sculptural, combining glass, wood, and even rock.

Combining solid wood with veneers and composites, along with modern adhesives and tooling, also has allowed makers unprecedented freedom of expression.

The examples we've included on the following pages taught us that even this most basic of furniture forms has continued to evolve in unexpected and often delightful directions.

Tsubo Coffee Table

Seth Rolland

Seth Rolland had a Japanese rock garden in mind when he designed this low table. He imagined the mahogany top as the gravel surface of the garden with the stone pushing upward through it. But, he adds, "You can look under the surface of this Japanese garden."

The design for the table came before Rolland actually had his hands on the rock. "The biggest challenge was that I had already determined the ideal height and width of the rock and then had to find one that was both that size and a beautiful shape and color," he says. He found the 90-lb. winner on a beach, a third of a mile from his car. In addition to its visual and textural qualities, the rock also has a practical purpose in balancing the table's cantilever.

Rolland, a professional from Port Townsend, Wash., has been making furniture for 18 years and now works in an 800-sq.-ft. studio next to his house.

"My work has evolved to be more organic in style and technique over time," Rolland says. Not surprisingly, two of his favorite artists are British sculptors David Nash and Andy Goldsworthy.

Size: 27 in. deep, 55 in. wide, 17 in. tall

Materials: Salvaged mahogany, stone

Finish: Thinned polyurethane

Contact: www.sethrolland.com

Monolith Sofa Table

Jari-Pekka Vilkman

Finnish furniture maker Jari-Pekka Vilkman works in a shop in Helsinki, but his two years at the College of the Redwoods in Fort Bragg, Calif., found a voice in this veneered sofa table.

"The idea behind my Coastline pieces is the north California coastline," Vilkman says. "The coastline is irregularly curved and drops down to the sea pretty much vertically. It really feels like the land's end there."

Vilkman had worked on a couple of dining tables and another sofa table in the same series, but wanted something more sculptural than his earlier pieces. After making a couple of rough sketches and a partial mock-up to define measurements, Vilkman had the design that would shape Monolith.

There were several practical hurdles to cross. One was the table's sheer size and weight. Another was the undulating veneer work along the edges and the carefully matched pattern on top. Finally, there was the high-gloss lacquer finish. "It was technically quite challenging," he says.

(Vilkman's lowboard appears on p. 142, and his East chair on p. 73.)

Size: 48 in. deep, 48 in. wide, 18 in. tall

Materials: Macassar ebony, ebony

Finish: Lacquer

Contact: www.j-pvilkman.com

Chicken Table

Thomas Schrunk

Thomas Schrunk says he was laughing most of the time he worked on his Three-Legged Chicken, a folding cocktail table (pun intended, he says) that can be wheeled into service on a set of casters.

The body is made from ½-in. medium-density fiberboard covered with figured maple veneers and a top of cherry veneer squares. The wings also are MDF veneered with figured maple, the feathers made from successive leaves of veneer. Three-Legged Chicken's head can be removed.

Schrunk describes himself as an "artist in lustrous materials." He has a woodworking studio in the arts district of Minneapolis but does his veneering at home in a basement shop that's friendlier to veneer. He was recently invited to make his fourth Steinway® Art Case piano.

"I decided to do this because I had never made a chicken table before," Schrunk says. "If I were to do this piece again I'd add a booby trap, a hidden tube of Ping-Pong® balls that would roll out of the back of the chicken when the head was touched."

Size: 54 in. deep, 56 in. wide, 16 in. tall

Materials: MDF, figured maple and cherry veneer, maple, bloodwood, locking casters

Finish: Catalyzed lacquer

Contact: www.lustracon.com

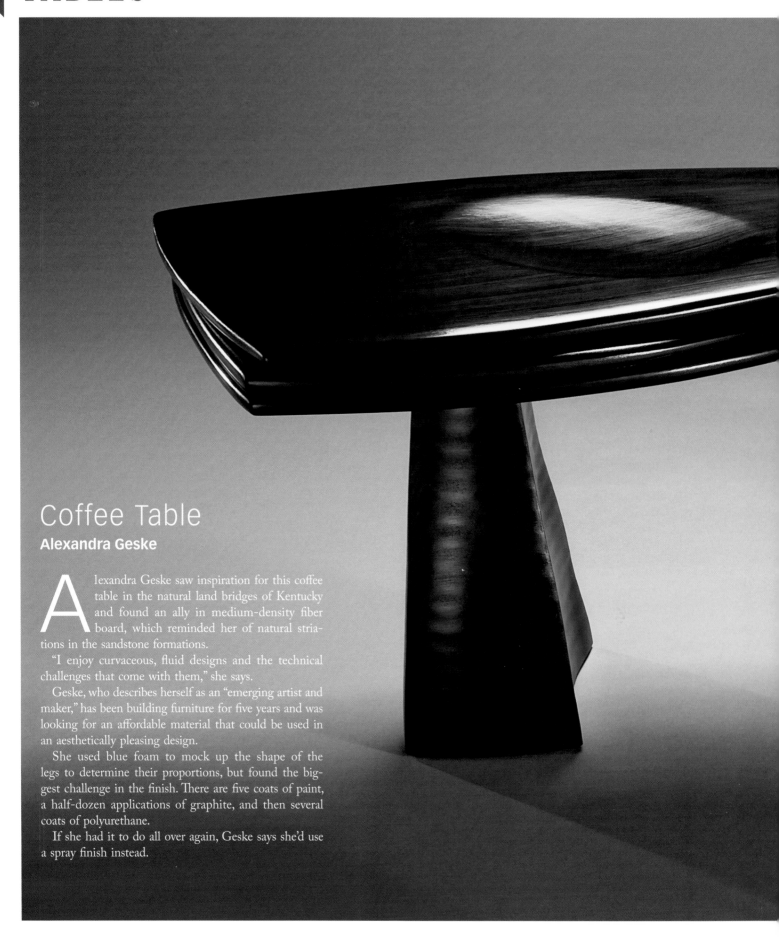

Coffee Table

Alexandra Geske

Alexandra Geske saw inspiration for this coffee table in the natural land bridges of Kentucky and found an ally in medium-density fiber board, which reminded her of natural striations in the sandstone formations.

"I enjoy curvaceous, fluid designs and the technical challenges that come with them," she says.

Geske, who describes herself as an "emerging artist and maker," has been building furniture for five years and was looking for an affordable material that could be used in an aesthetically pleasing design.

She used blue foam to mock up the shape of the legs to determine their proportions, but found the biggest challenge in the finish. There are five coats of paint, a half-dozen applications of graphite, and then several coats of polyurethane.

If she had it to do all over again, Geske says she'd use a spray finish instead.

Size: 22 in. deep., 48 in. wide, 18 in. tall

Materials: Medium-density fiberboard

Finish: Paint, graphite, polyurethane

Split-Top Table

Todd Partridge

Todd Partridge's goal was to design a small table in which the top did not obscure the base. His answer was to allow a series of wedge-shaped frames that make up the base to extend all the way through the tabletop.

"I find that the challenge of building small tables is that the top obscures the underlying structure," he says. "Using a piece of glass would have been the easy way out, and I struggled to find an alternative way that would integrate the top with the base. By opening the top, visual access to the underlying structure is achieved."

Partridge is the master artist-in-residence at the Appalachian Artisan Center in Hindman, Ky. A furniture maker since 1992, Partridge says much of his work "explores structural and functional form."

Size: 23 in. dia., 23 in. tall

Materials: Bleached ash

Finish: Lacquer

Contact: www.toddpartridgedesign.com

Cirque Hall Table

Nick Boynton

"I wanted a table design which conveyed an energy or tension," says Missoula, Mont., furniture maker Nick Boynton. "Mass would defeat this emphasis, so I concentrated on form, line, and negative space."

Until Boynton's first gallery show in 1997, he worked mainly on commission for clients with design ideas of their own. But since then, he has been making furniture exclusively to be sold in galleries and based on his own designs. Those, he says, are a "derivative of Oriental aesthetics."

Boynton works from a series of small sketches, several on a single page, that eventually become a montage of ideas. He does full-scale drawings when joinery looks to be especially tricky, as is the case here where the arching rails meet the curved, inwardly sloping leg panels. Overall, Boynton says he's pleased with the outcome and is working on a dining table that springs from the same design.

Size: 24 in. deep, 54 in. long, 18 in. tall

Materials: Maple, cherry

Finish: Catalyzed lacquer

Contact: www.nwfinewoodworking.com

Core Sample 10

Matt Hutton

Maine furniture maker Matt Hutton explains that the title for this table comes from the cylindrical extractions of soil or ice that a scientist might take in the course of research.

"I use this term because of its inherent reference toward time, history, and layers, all of which are characteristics of my primary medium, wood," Hutton writes. "This term is also used because of its suggestion of parts, pieces, fossils, and information on structure and construction."

Starting with rough sketches but no prototype, Hutton says he worked out construction as he went. Figuring out how to assemble the slats with intentional irregularity and keep fasteners hidden was a major challenge. "There was a lot of time spent problem-solving during the construction of this piece," he says.

Hutton works in a 1,000-sq.-ft. studio located at his home in Portland, Maine. The building also houses a studio for his wife, a painter.

Size: 9 in. deep, 29 in. wide, 29 in. tall

Materials: Fir, ash

Finish: Leather dye and oil

Contact: www.studio24b.com

Coffee Table

Gary Rogowski

Gary Rogowski draws from a deep design well when he builds furniture. Influences include Wharton Esherick, Greene and Greene, James Krenov, Charles Rennie Mackintosh, and Chinese designers of centuries ago whose names he doesn't even know.

All of those elements may be represented in this low table, but Rogowski says it really sprang from a desk he was working on and, in particular, its shapely legs. He adapted the ideas to coffee-table height, making these arched legs from 4-in.-thick stock. That still wasn't beefy enough to get the full shape without gluing on extra pieces above the knee. These wings, Rogowski says, were actually the scraps left over after cutting the profile in the lower part of the legs. When the pieces were joined to create the whole leg, the grain match was flawless.

The layered top is made of three sections, a 1-in.-thick top with a deep rabbet along the bottom edge, and then two additional frames below it.

Rogowski is a self-taught professional who has been making furniture since 1974. He is the director of the Northwest Woodworking Studio, which he founded in Portland, Ore., a decade ago. He is also a writer and a contributing editor for *Fine Woodworking* magazine.

His school and shop are located in a 100-year-old horse stable close to the center of the city. "It's a mess," he writes of his working environment. "Clutter, I convince myself, is the sign of a fertile mind."

Size: 30 in. deep, 48 in. wide, 18 in. tall

Materials: Mahogany

Finish: Stain, oil, and wax

Contact: www.northwestwoodworking.com

Pair of Side Tables

Timothy Coleman

Some especially attractive tiger maple was one of the design seeds for these side tables by Timothy Coleman. He wanted to explore the possibilities of composing squares of veneer parquet style, producing this checkerboard-like appearance with wood all of the same color.

The veneer is laid up on a plywood substrate with solid-wood borders, giving Coleman the material he needed to give the edge its sculpted profile. "The idea was to create a strong table base that had slender, curving parts and have the top appear to slightly float above it," Coleman says.

If the tabletop draws most of the attention, it was actually this base that was the most difficult detail to work out. Coleman made a full-scale model of the leg in poplar to resolve the degree of taper and how much the leg kicked in at the bottom. "The biggest challenge was to get the table base to have the right degree of 'springiness' without being visually wimpy or structurally unsound," he says.

Coleman is a member of the New Hampshire Furniture Masters Association who has taken design clues from a number of sources, including Art Deco designers, furniture makers James Krenov, Kristina Madsen, Hank Gilpin, and John Dunnigan, and both sculpture and Asian pattern-making. (His upholstered settee appears on p. 65.)

Coleman works in a 1,000-sq.-ft. studio next to his home in Shelburne, Mass., where furniture making is "delightfully woven into the fabric of family life."

Size: 22 in. deep, 22 in. wide, 24 in. tall

Materials: Walnut, plywood, tiger maple

Finish: Tung oil-urethane mix

Contact: www.timothycoleman.com

Coffee Table
Alexandria Reznikoff

Alexandria Reznikoff had been making furniture for just over a year and was a student at the Center for Furniture Craftsmanship in Maine when she built this table for an assignment on bending, laminating, and veneering.

"When I thought of this, for some reason I thought of a worn piece of paper," she writes, "and I wanted to re-create that as sculpture."

Reznikoff conferred with instructors Tim Rousseau and Tom Harrington on how to bend the plywood core of the top without breaking it. But a more significant hurdle was the design of the legs, which Reznikoff says took several tries.

In fact, the solution was an accident. As instructors and classmates commented on one possible leg design, Reznikoff says, "We just grabbed something to hold up the other side of the top. Turns out it was a perfect match."

Reznikoff is now working out of her garage in Florida but says she'd like to work with others in a co-operative shop.

Size: 24 in. deep, 48 in. wide, 15 in. tall

Materials: Bending plywood, mahogany veneer

Finish: Polyurethane

Contact: www.woodbyalex.com

Interlocking Tables

Chris Bach

A modernist piece designed by Edward Wormley and manufactured by the Dunbar company in the mid-1950s helped Chris Bach with his version of interlocking tables. "I've always been drawn to modular pieces," Bach says, "and I try to create objects that can stand alone as well as work in a system. It was important that this could be arranged as a right- or left-facing L as well."

Coincidentally, Wormley, who died in 1995, got his start in Chicago, where Bach is working. He is apprenticing as a chairmaker with Jeff Miller as he builds his own business.

Bach says he has drawn more on architectural influences and industrial design than on the work of specific furniture makers, looking to subway trains, graphic design, and poster art of the 20th century.

Bach's current interest is chairs. "Since I've started building chairs, I've shifted from focusing solely on how furniture relates to its environment and have become more conscious of how it relates to the human body," Bach says. "Stylewise, this has drawn me to slip a couple of compound angles and curves into the mix."

Size: 15 in. deep, 72 in. wide, 21 in. tall; 24 in. deep, 40 in. wide, 18 in. tall

Materials: Red oak

Finish: Aniline dye, oil, wax

Contact: www.bachcustomjoinery.com

Dining Table

Roger Heitzman

California furniture maker Roger Heitzman says he leans toward Art Nouveau and Art Deco styles. Those influences are at work in this dining table, which Heitzman describes as a way of giving a "curvilinear interpretation of Arts and Crafts style."

A furniture maker for 31 years, Heitzman is anything but hidebound. This mahogany and wenge table started as a hand-drawn sketch but blossomed with CAD modeling and computer renderings that could make it look just as real as a photograph.

Heitzman earned a degree in architecture and later opened his own drafting company. But a visit to a furniture exhibit at the San Diego County Fair in the mid-1970s proved a turning point. He went back to school, got a degree in industrial design, and later taught school.

Eventually, he moved to the Santa Cruz area and took up furniture making full time.

His multipurpose professional background may help explain an unusual talent for making tools as well as furniture. He has fashioned a number of stationary power tools—including a bandsaw, a tablesaw, and a complicated router duplication machine.

Size: 40 in. deep, 84 in. wide, 29 in. tall

Materials: Mahogany, wenge

Finish: Polyurethane

Contact: www.heitzmanstudios.com

TABLES

Computer Center
Kay Selle

K ay Selle wanted a command center for computers, telephones, and other equipment that could, in a pinch, be used for a formal dining table. Her design incorporates laminate, ¼-in. plywood, and even a section of a 36-in.-dia. concrete form—all in keeping with an aim to keep woodworking practical.

"I like utilitarian pieces that can stand up to abuse," she says. "I try to use more pedestrian materials like laminate and veneer plywood in combination with solid wood and metal. I don't like to use materials that are so precious that people are afraid of ruining them."

Selle worked as a fashion designer before her four children came along, and she finds similarities between constructing garments and building furniture. She works in a garage workshop during her spare time (that is, when her children are in school).

The only spot in the house that could accommodate a home tech center of this size was the family's dining room, so that's where it went. On demand, it will comfortably seat a dozen people for dinner.

Size: 82 in. dia., 30 in. tall

Materials: Laminate over particleboard core, birch plywood, pine, stainless steel, Sonotube® concrete form

Finish: Stain, Waterlox®

Contact: kay@selledesign.com

Kay Selle used a 3-ft.-dia. concrete form as the core for this computer center. With walls nearly ½ in. thick, the form has the density of hardboard and proved an ample foundation for the work center built around it.

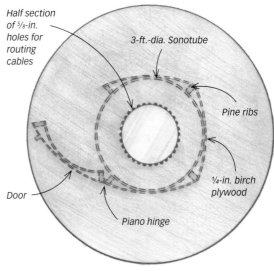

Half section of ⅝-in. holes for routing cables

3-ft.-dia. Sonotube

Pine ribs

¼-in. birch plywood

Door

Piano hinge

Low Tea Table

Michael Cullen

This low table began when one of Michael Cullen's students gave him a beautiful piece of claro walnut. He knew right away that the wood should become a table, most likely in the style of a type of Chinese table used for a game called Wei-Ch'i.

But the trick was to interfere as little as possible with what the wood already was.

"I like to think of it as keeping the tree in the wood, as opposed to removing that quality through the process of making lumber," Cullen says. "With this particular type of work I find that the challenge is to create a natural piece that looks untouched by technique or tools. Of course, this piece is highly stylized in some sense, but upon viewing it I want the focus to be on the natural beauty and not what I have done to it." (A chest by Cullen appears on p. 128.)

Size: 25 in. deep, 25 in. wide, 9 in. tall

Materials: Claro walnut

Finish: Tung oil on top and feet; live edge burnished and waxed

Contact: www.michaelcullendesign.com

Nightstand

Jeff O'Brien

Jeff O'Brien built this nightstand as a class assignment for the Northwest Woodworking Studio in Portland, Ore. Still working an outside job and with a sizable workload, O'Brien thought he'd be able to knock off the nightstand quickly.

Turns out he was wrong. O'Brien found the finger joints were more work that he had bargained for. He eventually built a router-table sled and some precise gauge blocks to help him through the process.

Working from a rough sketch, O'Brien built a scale model to check proportions and to make sure he liked the legs.

O'Brien is just launching a professional furniture-making career after 20 years as a video editor. "I just couldn't see myself sitting behind a computer screen for the next 20," he says. "I had been making programs and commercials that had a very short life span, so I wanted to start creating some work that might be around a good bit longer." (O'Brien's Cord Chair appears on p. 60.)

Size: 20 in. deep, 17¼ in. wide, 34½ in. tall

Materials: Cherry, ebonized ash, walnut

Finish: Oil-varnish mix

Contact: www.dogwood-design.com

Gift from the Tree

John Marckworth

This coffee table began with a 10-ft. plank of bubinga that John Marckworth stumbled across in Port Townsend, Wash. "I knew I had to build something with it," Marckworth says. "I considered several possibilities but decided a coffee table would best serve to display the wood."

For all of its beauty, the bubinga was a tough-to-work combination of figured heartwood and spalted sapwood. Marckworth used cyanoacrylate glue to fill and stabilize the surface before applying a finish.

From a design standpoint, Marckworth found his biggest challenge in the size and proportions of the reverse-taper legs. "After sketches and drawings, I made ⅛-in. plywood mock-ups and experimented with proto-types until I was satisfied," he says.

Marckworth, the co-founder of the Port Townsend School of Woodworking, is a self-taught furniture maker who still spends most of his time professionally as a cabinetmaker. He squeezes in furniture nights and weekends in his 975-sq.-ft. basement shop. "Furniture making," he says, "is therapy."

Size: 26 in. deep, 53 in. wide, 17 in. tall

Materials: Bubinga, painted poplar

Finish: Polyurethane

Contact: www.marckworthdesign.com

Maple Tri-Angle Table

David Hogan

David Hogan, a wood technology instructor at Fullerton College in California, used repetitive geometric shapes to create a table that reflects his interest in contemporary furniture designs.

Working from sketches, Hogan says he used ⅛-in. cardboard to arrive at the final shape of the triangles. "The biggest challenge was determining the proper angles that would allow the triangles to be joined together," he says. "After that, I had to angle all of the other edges so that the base footprint would also be a triangle."

The components are made from Baltic-birch plywood veneered with maple in a vacuum press. Hogan ironed veneer to the edges to hide the plies.

Hogan, who studied furniture making at the North Bennet Street School in Boston, works in Fullerton's shop, mainly on his teaching breaks.

Size: Top 30 in. dia., 29½ in. tall

Materials: Maple veneered Baltic-birch plywood

Finish: Wood dye, lacquer

Contact: dhogan@fullcoll.edu

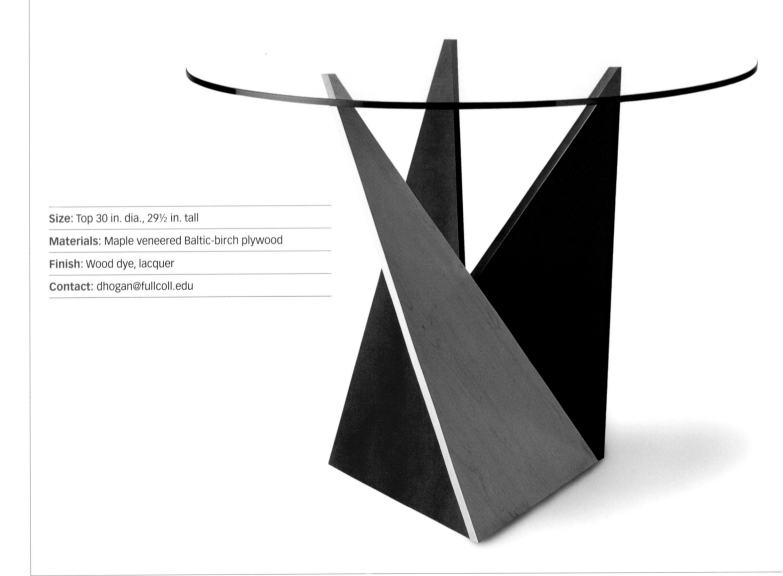

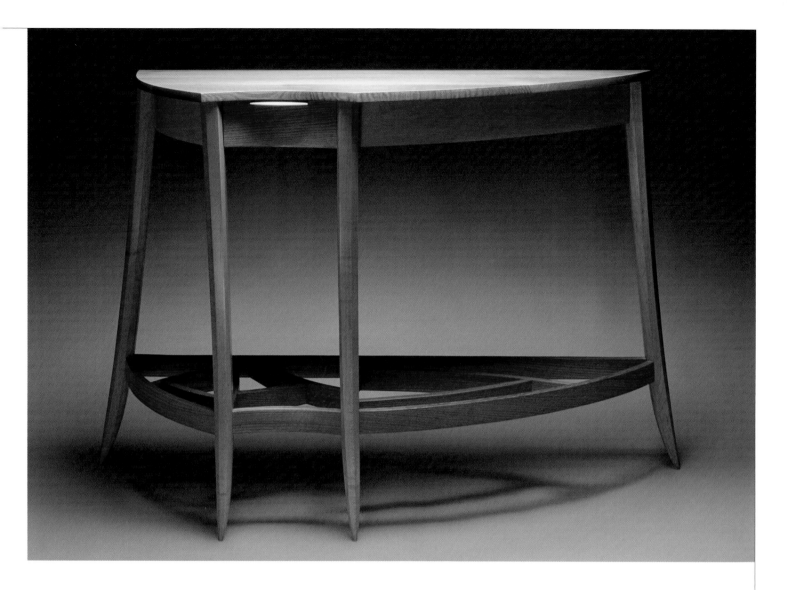

Hall Table

Leah Woods

Leah Woods designed this hall table after completing the vanity and matching chair that appear on p. 125. "That piece was such a long process, from the idea through technique, experimentation with form, etc." Woods writes. "After finishing the table and chair, I was really happy with the forms and wanted to continue experimenting with what I saw as broad, sweeping curves. But I wanted to build a simpler piece."

Given its simple function and manageable size, a hall table seemed to offer the right opportunity, Woods says.

She chose white oak and maple for their subtle contrast. The drawer is lined with African satinwood, a very bright yellow that Woods says relates well to the brass hardware.

Size: 23 in. deep, 59 in. wide, 42 in. tall

Materials: Maple, white oak, African satinwood, brass

Finish: Lacquer

Contact: www.leahwoodsstudio.com

Stucks' Table

David Upfill-Brown

At 5 ft. wide and 10 ft. long, David Upfill-Brown's oval dining table melds structural stability, interference-free seating for diners, and the graceful lines of classical furniture.

It was Upfill-Brown's fourth table of similar design. Two were shorter, one longer, but none quite as successful. The three earlier designs did, however, give Upfill-Brown a chance to see how the overall length of the top affected the curves of the legs. "Previously," he writes, "these did not please me as much as this one does. Ten foot is the length that best accommodates the curves."

Upfill-Brown points out that even an interesting table can go unappreciated in a small room when the understructure is lost to view. In this case, his clients' house had an open-plan living area, so all parts of the table are visible.

Although Upfill-Brown had intended to shape the legs from solid cherry, he worried that short grain sections would be inherently weak and that the process would produce too much waste. Instead, he made each pair of legs from plantation-grown poplar and veneered them with cherry. (A box made by Upfill-Brown appears on pp. 152-153.)

Size: 60 in. deep, 120 in. wide, 30 in. tall

Materials: North American cherry, poplar

Finish: Conversion varnish

1/16-in. veneer glued on
tapered laminations

Dowels to rail

End grain end cap

Top short leg
(minor axis)

Top long leg
(major axis)

Grooves for splines

Veneer

Plywood splines

The laminated and
veneered base for this
dining table by David
Upfill-Brown springs
from a four-way miter at
the center of the table.
The four pieces that
make up the upper and
lower frames are joined
with plywood splines.

Ikebana Table

Kevin Rodel

Kevin Rodel doesn't have to think long and hard about who has been the single most important influence on his work, nor should anyone else who is familiar with Charles Rennie Mackintosh, the Scottish-born architect, designer, and eventual giant of the Arts and Crafts movement. "Can't you tell?" Rodel asks.

Rodel calls this piece the Ikebana Table, after the Japanese art of displaying cut flowers in a way that emphasizes line and form rather than blooms. He says the table is well-suited to displaying a variety of art objects, and adds that he has already modified the design for future commissions where it will become a desk, a hall table, and a low table for a high-definition television. "Interestingly," Rodel writes, "that last one brings it full circle. Since most TVs are made in Japan, it seems appropriate to display the flower of 21st-century technology on it."

Until last year, Rodel's shop was in rural Pownal, Maine, but he has since moved to Fort Andross, a refurbished textile mill on the banks of the Androscoggin River in nearby Brunswick. He is close to other businesses and artists and within walking distance of where he lives.

Working by himself and with a mix of hand and power tools, Rodel uses mostly native hardwoods and avoids the incorporation of turnings in his pieces. He has a looser design style than many of his peers, starting with sketches and eventually moving to scaled drawings, but never employing full-scale drawings or mockups. Linseed oil or shellac finishes are correspondingly simple, even if the furniture forms are not. "I'm pretty basic low-tech," he says.

Size: 20 in. deep, 82 in. wide, 28½ in. tall

Materials: Cherry, cypress, glass

Finish: Shellac

Contact: www.kevinrodel.com

Side Table
Aurelio Bolognesi

This table by Aurelio Bolognesi followed an invitation to join the New Hampshire Furniture Masters Association, whose annual fall auction showcases some of the best current work anywhere. "I wanted to make a piece that would be clean and innovative, yet with enough technical subtleties to fit in such a prestigious group," Bolognesi says.

The design, he says, was a "natural evolution" of previous work, including two dressers and a small table that had similar detailing in the legs and the undercut of the top.

The biggest challenge here, he says, was attaching the aprons to the angled legs in such a way that the mortises didn't weaken the legs.

Bolognesi, a furniture maker for 40 years, graduated from a design school in Switzerland and apprenticed in woodworking shops in both Switzerland and France. "I began by sweeping a furniture maker's shop as a little boy," he says.

He is in the process of moving into a new shop in Hardwick, Mass., which he says will include a large storage area for lumber and a separate finishing area. With more of his work involving lumber starting in log form, the storage area will be especially welcome.

Size: 18 in. deep, 60 in. wide, 33 in. tall

Materials: Quartersawn and flatsawn cherry (all from the same log)

Finish: French polish

Contact: www.aurelio-bolognesi.com

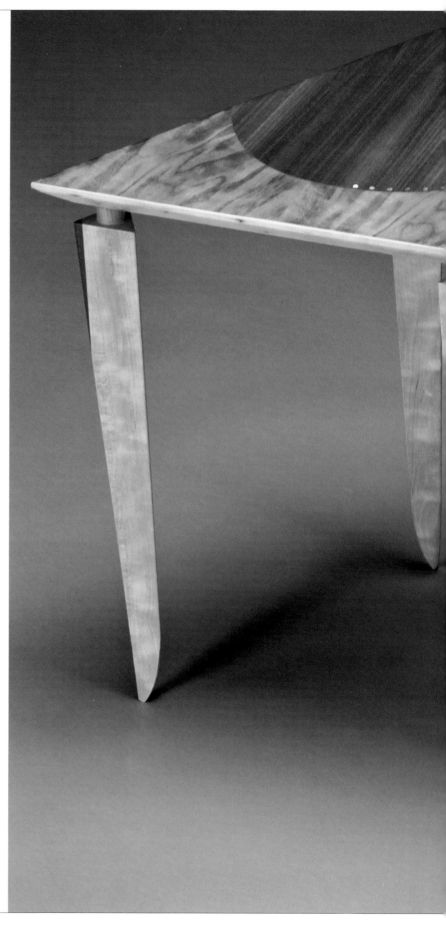

Flexible Coffee Table

Brian Bortz

Brian Bortz had been making this occasional table for years and thought it would make a good foundation for a flexible coffee table whose three components could be used separately or arranged together.

A major construction challenge was developing a secure leg-to-top connection. The solution is a "mushroomed" joint that firmly anchors the top of a connecting dowel in a bed of epoxy (see drawing).

"The design challenge," Bortz adds, "was creating marquetry work across the top so the three tables flowed together as I wanted them to. Aligning all the tips was too geometric for me, so I designed the marquetry to flow when the tables are offset slightly from each other."

Bortz is a 10-year professional whose formal training consists of seminars he's taken with furniture makers Michael Fortune, Garrett Hack, and Victor DiNovi. He works in a 3,000-sq.-ft. cooperative shop in a Durham, N.C., warehouse with one other furniture maker.

Size: 19 in. deep, 37 in. wide, 21 in. tall (arranged as shown)

Materials: Cherry (legs); bloodwood, walnut, cherry (tops); Paua abalone (accents)

Finish: Water-based conversion varnish

Contact: www.lostartwoodworks.com

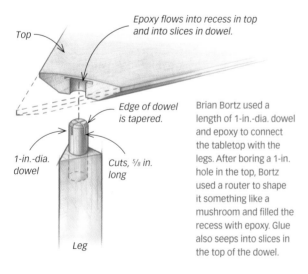

Epoxy flows into recess in top and into slices in dowel.

Top

Edge of dowel is tapered.

1-in.-dia. dowel

Cuts, 5/8 in. long

Leg

Brian Bortz used a length of 1-in.-dia. dowel and epoxy to connect the tabletop with the legs. After boring a 1-in. hole in the top, Bortz used a router to shape it something like a mushroom and filled the recess with epoxy. Glue also seeps into slices in the top of the dowel.

Coffee Table

Jon Siegel

You'd never guess by looking at this low table, but for years, New Hampshire furniture maker Jon Siegel built in the early American style—gate-leg tables and banister-back chairs. "Once I got the big lathe," he says, "I jumped three centuries and started with contemporary forms."

He suspects he was remembering the work of Stephen Hogbin, who 35 years ago was cutting massive turnings into furniture forms.

Siegel's 1,200-sq.-ft. shop houses a number of lathes, including one that can handle work weighing 2½ tons. This table started as a 4-ft.-dia. blank of mahogany weighing more than 100 lb.

Siegel says that while his work now consists exclusively of turnings, he still has a complete woodworking shop as well as a metal shop with three screw-turning lathes. He goes directly from idea to 1:12 scale model without benefit of any drawings. When he gets close to a final design, he'll make one larger model, then the project.

"At the time I made this piece, it was the largest-diameter work I had ever done," he says. It sold at a New Hampshire Furniture Masters auction.

Size: 26 in. deep, 56 in. wide (top)

Materials: Mahogany, glass

Finish: Oil and wax

Contact: www.bigtreeturnings.com

Emergence
Thomas Monahan

Thomas Monahan calls this low table Emergence, and its curved, form-bent legs proved his biggest construction challenge. The legs are made from layers of tapered Baltic-birch plywood glued on a form and then trimmed to size and mortised for the curved stretcher.

"Emergence is an energetic and engaging piece that portrays wood as a living, moving, and pliable medium," Monahan says.

Monahan used Delrin® plastic spacers and aluminum bars to connect the legs to the top. "When complete," he says, "the tabletop appears to rest on the spacers and float ¼ in. above the legs."

Monahan has been making furniture for 20 years, although furniture is not his full-time occupation. He works as a custom cabinetmaker in Cedar Rapids, Iowa.

Size: 20¼ in. deep, 48¼ in. wide, 16 in. tall

Materials: Wenge, English sycamore veneer, plywood, padauk

Finish: Urethane

Contact: thomasjmonahan@imonmail.com

Console Table
with Shelves

Paul Stefanski

Both architect and furniture maker, Paul Stefanski is interested in the place where abstract design meets functionality. "I am always looking for a clear and simple way of providing the necessities of a piece," he says. "In the case of the console table, this is exemplified by using a single piece of wood to create a foot, shelves, and a tabletop."

Stefanski had originally designed a series of wall-mounted shelves before adapting the idea to freestanding pieces. He chose a miter joint to emphasize the continuity of the wood, as if it were being folded around corners. He designed the double-tenon miter joint to go along with it.

Stefanski, who studied at the Center for Furniture Craftsmanship in Maine, has been making furniture for 10 years. He has been renting 1,200 sq. ft. of warehouse space but is in the process of relocating his shop to the garage of the house he and his wife purchased in Wauwatosa, Wis.

"Although I enjoy the romance of hand tools," he says, "I am increasingly using power tools for my joinery because of their speed and accuracy."

Size: 11 in. deep, 44 in. wide, 34 in. tall

Materials: Ash, black walnut

Finish: Oil-varnish blend

Contact: www.paulstefanski.com

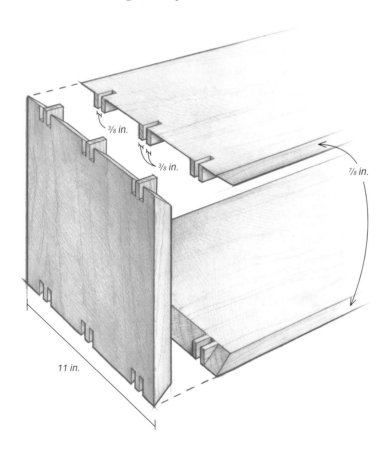

Paul Stefanski wanted to use miter joints to assemble his console table, but reinforcing them with splines after assembly would have been all but impossible. Instead, Stefanski came up with this joint, which combines miters with pairs of integral tenons.

Honu Coffee Table

Peter Loh

Peter Loh says the design inspiration for this coffee table grew out of a backpacking trip in Hawaii where he watched a green sea turtle (or "honu") swimming in a shallow pool of water. "The flowing lines and beauty of the turtle suspended in the water inspired the creation of Honu," Loh says.

Loh, from Bellevue, Wash., has been making furniture for 11 years and says his designs are based on experiences and forms found in nature. "Over the years the work has taken on more organic shapes and become more fluid," he says. "At present my latest designs mark an attempt to blur the lines between sculpture and functional object."

Once he had settled on the flipper-like shape of the legs for this low table, Loh took to the computer, where he used CAD software to produce full-scale drawings.

Loh studied photography in art school and found himself in a woodworking workshop in the summer of his last year of graduate school. "I designed and built a chair there," he says. "It was totally liberating to make something both useful and attractive. I was hooked."

Size: 30 in. deep, 48 in. wide, 20 in. tall

Materials: Bubinga and cocobolo

Finish: Varnish, wax

Contact: www.peterloh.com

Oceana Console

Paulus Wanrooij

Paulus Wanrooij got the idea for a series of tables with similar bases after experimenting with strips of $\frac{1}{16}$-in.-thick veneer. "Of course they bend and curve very easily and that is how it started," he says. "The leg of this table was first used in the Oceana end table. Since then it has been applied to support various-size tops—round, triangular, rectangle, demilune, and console."

A professional furniture maker in Woolwich, Maine, Wanrooij has been making furniture for six years and says his style is still developing. His shop is a two-car garage next to the house.

Wanrooij comes to furniture making from a business career. He previously worked in telecom and mail order. "I feel that the most important thing is focus," he says. "Don't give up, never let go. I work seven days a week and I handle every aspect of the furniture business, including marketing and administration."

Size: 19 in. deep, 42 in. wide, 32 in. tall

Materials: Walnut, sapele, maple

Finish: Legs in lacquer, top in tung oil and polyurethane

Contact: www.paulusfurniture.com

Ash and Cherry Table

John Godfrey II

The figured cherry top may be the most visible element of this table, but it was the legs and understructure that had maker John Godfrey scratching his head. "The compound angles involved with the joinery of this table proved to be the most challenging part of its construction," Godfrey says.

Godfrey, who is enrolled in the Fellowship Program at the Center for Furniture Craftsmanship in Rockport, Maine, knew the legs would be the key to the table. "I focused on their appearance the most," he says, "sketching until I achieved the proper form."

Although he typically works from full-scale drawings, Godfrey says the table's lack of right angles and its organic form made them less useful in this instance. He made a ¼-scale model of the table before launching into the real thing.

Godfrey steam-bent the legs using a technique developed by William Keyser Jr. and laminated the aprons. But he says he would saw them from solid wood if he were to make the table again. "Although laminations yield a consistent result," he says, "sawn solid wood is more time effective."

Size: 19 in. deep, 43 in. wide, 33 in. tall

Materials: Ebonized ash, figured cherry

Finish: Oil-varnish

Bloodwood Perspective Top Table

Thomas Schrunk

Roman mosaic patterns that Thomas Schrunk had seen while working as an archaeological photographer were the starting point for the perspective pattern of this tabletop.

Schrunk made a full-size drawing of the inner section of the pattern and cut pieces of veneer to fit before adding the border. "The underside of the table has a similar design, though simpler," Schrunk adds, "something of a signature of mine."

A major challenge was finding bloodwood stock for the legs beefier than 4/4. In the end, Schrunk glued up the legs. He says he was careful to use quartersawn material from the edges of boards to minimize the possibility that the legs would bow or twist later. (Schrunk's Chicken Table appears on p. 9.)

Size: 24 in. deep, 24 in. wide, 24 in. tall

Materials: Bloodwood, maple, sapele and bloodwood veneers

Finish: Catalyzed lacquer

Contact: www.lustracon.com

Akira Dining Set

Hank Holzer

Hank Holzer named this table and chair dining set after Yoshizawa Akira, the Japanese origami master who died in 2005 at the age of 94. Akira is credited with developing a wet-folding technique that allowed a more rounded style of paperfolding.

Holzer says he began developing the Akira chair five years ago after he got tired of chairs with four legs and a back. "I'm always surprised by the ability of this chair to hold up," he adds. "We use one daily and I weigh 180 lb. I'm not particularly delicate with it, though I don't recommend my customers stand on it like I do in my demos."

He attributes the surprising strength of these designs to a splined miter joint cut with extremely close tol-

erances and assembled with structural epoxy and very strong spline stock.

Holzer shares a 4,000-sq.-ft. shop in Seattle with his wife and five other full- and part-time woodworkers. "I tried working in a solo shop and lasted for about a year before moving into a group shop," he says. "I was so lonely."

Size: Table: 42 in. deep, 76 in. wide, 30 in. tall; Chair: 22 in. deep, 18 in. wide, 33 in. tall

---

Materials: Urban harvested spalted cherry, jatoba, wenge

Finish: Conversion varnish

Contact: www.nwfinewoodworking.com

Elm Wave

Celia Greiner

The idea for this bench/table came from a sculpture incorporating a wave shape that its maker thought could be translated into a piece of furniture with multiple uses. Celia Greiner says her biggest challenge was not letting its sculptural qualities take the upper hand.

"I used to make sculptural furniture that was too complex and not too comfortable and that perhaps had too much personality," Greiner writes. "I have learned to simplify the designs and make furniture that is, first of all, a piece of functioning furniture and, secondly, not only looks good but begs to be touched."

Greiner, who works from an 800-sq.-ft. shop on Chicago's west side, shapes wood with an arsenal of power and hand tools that includes everything from a bandsaw to microplanes. She says she normally works from full-scale drawings but in this case used a simple sketch and went ahead without a prototype.

"I threw all caution to the wind," she says.

Size: 12 in. deep, 43 in. wide, 14½ in. tall

Materials: Elm, walnut

Finish: Oil and wax

Contact: www.celiagreiner.com

Game Table

Kevin Gill

The commission for this game table brought with it a long list of conditions: It had to incorporate boards for both backgammon and chess; the chess squares were to measure 1½ in. square to fit the homeowner's chess set; the table could be made only from maple; and, not least, it would have to work with two Sting chairs designed by Gijs Papavoine.

Undeterred, Kevin Gill produced this table with a reversible top, often braving Maine snowstorms to meet the deadline and driving in the middle of the night to use the facilities at the Center for Furniture Craftsmanship, where he was enrolled in the Fellowship program.

The backgammon board was especially challenging because Gill was limited to maple veneer. To create enough contrast between three distinct but adjoining areas, he tested a number of combinations before settling on curly maple, flatsawn maple, and yellow birch. ("Yes," he says, "I cheated with the yellow birch, but the designer and homeowner didn't mind.")

Gill is quick to credit several others for their help, including Peter Korn at the center, Aled Lewis, a former instructor, Gregg Lipton's Gazelle Table, and Donna Janville, the interior designer who provided the specs.

"I think there's incredible value for a furniture maker in working on commissioned projects," Gill says. "They can force you out of your comfort zone and through obstacles that you might otherwise seek to circumvent."

Size: 32 in. deep, 32 in. wide, 29 in. tall

Materials: Maple, maple veneers, birch veneer, medium-density fiberboard, aluminum dowels

Finish: Conversion varnish

Contact: www.kevingillstudios.com

Trestle Table

Tyler Chartier

Tyler Chartier's trestle-style dining table combines his appreciation for Shaker and Arts and Crafts furniture with his use of curves to complement the figure of wood.

"I have come to appreciate more classic, simple designs," says Chartier, a five-year professional.

Chartier started learning the craft in his father's woodshop. Later, his grandfather gave him some of his tools after Chartier abandoned a suit-and-tie career for a furniture maker's life. His "glorified garage shop" of 600 sq. ft. is located in a forested region north of California's wine country.

Chartier says he starts his designs on paper and then moves to a computer where he creates virtual mock-ups. His CAD program can produce the measured drawings

he needs for construction. The process may be high-tech, but Chartier uses a mix of hand and power tools and says the top on this table was flattened mainly with handplanes.

Design, not actual construction, was the major part of the table as Chartier looked for a way to "use negative space to lighten the trestle without making it seem structurally weak."

Size: 36 in. deep, 69 in. wide, 30 in. tall

Materials: Canary and jatoba

Finish: Custom oil mix

Contact: www.chartiercustomfurniture.com

Display Table
Rick Gorman

Rick Gorman says he was originally drawn to Stickley style furniture: substantial, heavy pieces in dark oak. "Now," he says, "I like a much lighter style and use color and texture to create different effects."

That may be partly due to Gorman's two-year apprenticeship with Michael Cullen (see Cullen's painted chest on p. 128) as well as his own evolution as a furniture maker.

Gorman has been making furniture for 25 years, five of them as a professional. He now works as a banker. His shop is an 8-ft. by 12-ft. shed in the backyard.

Gorman built this sprightly table from full-scale drawings. He began with a small sketch of the curved legs, moved to larger drawings, then sample pieces, and finally a full-size mock-up. Other than trying the table in a different species of wood, he wouldn't change anything in the design.

Size: 16 in. deep, 11 in. wide, 32½ in. tall

Materials: Ash

Finish: Shellac

Contact: rgorman3916@aol.com

Ross Table
Bob Kopf

I f it hadn't been for a bout of bursitis that forced a change in work habits, along with an introduction to copper boat-building rivets, Bob Kopf might have taken a completely different direction with this tall entry table. As it turned out, circumstances helped Kopf explore some new design avenues. Prompted to work with lighter materials, he found that he liked them.

He used his 20-in. bandsaw to rip oak into quartersawn slats for the top. The framework of the table base is joined with rivets he learned how to use at the North Carolina Watercraft Center.

Kopf is a self-taught professional who has been making furniture for 35 years. His shop, located in rural Stokes County, N.C., is a 24-ft. by 36-ft. building he put up 25 years ago right next door to his house.

An admirer of George Nakashima, Wharton Esherick, Art Carpenter, Wendell Castle, John Makepeace, and the Shakers, Kopf says: "As my skills have matured, the work has gotten lighter and more crisp."

Size: 17½ in. deep, 42 in. wide, 37 in. tall

Materials: Curly chestnut oak, walnut, copper rivets

Finish: Wax

Contact: BobKopfww@msn.com

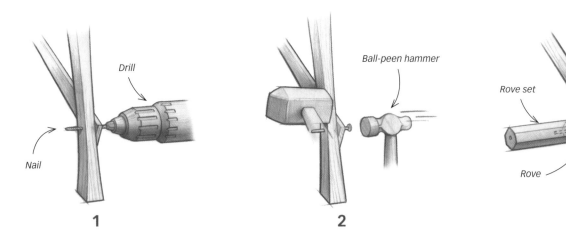

1 — Nail, Drill

2 — Ball-peen hammer

3 — Rove set, Rove

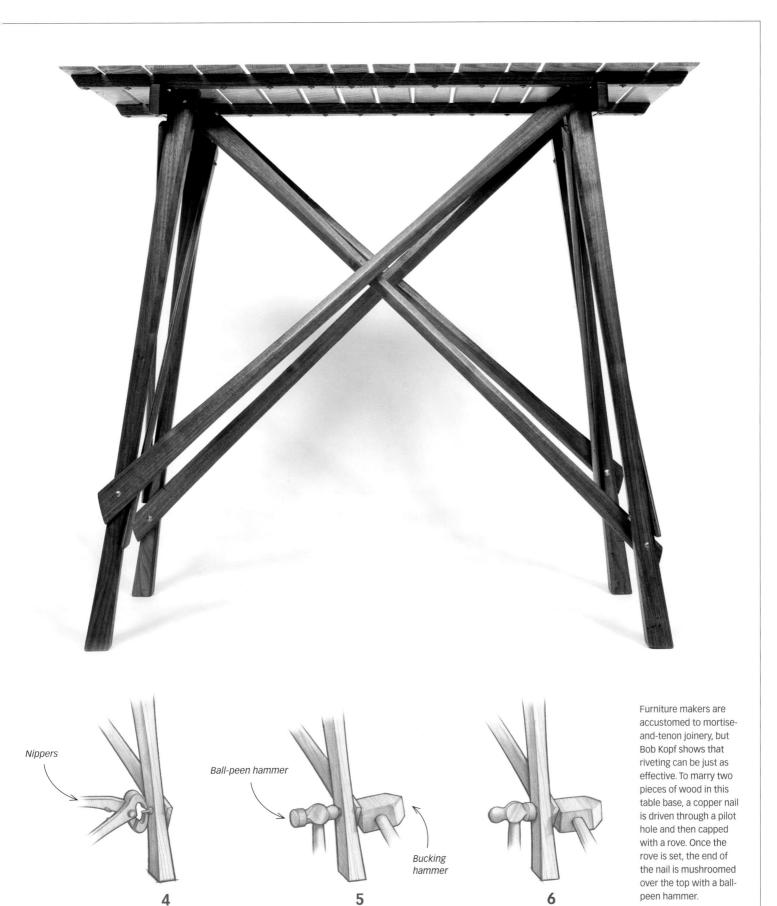

Nippers

Ball-peen hammer

Bucking hammer

4

5

6

Furniture makers are accustomed to mortise-and-tenon joinery, but Bob Kopf shows that riveting can be just as effective. To marry two pieces of wood in this table base, a copper nail is driven through a pilot hole and then capped with a rove. Once the rove is set, the end of the nail is mushroomed over the top with a ball-peen hammer.

BEDS

Beds, or bedsteads as elaborate versions once were called, were prized possessions of American settlers. But the familiar four-posters with canopies of decorative fabric were the province of the well-to-do. Working families made do with simple wooden frames or even straw-stuffed ticks arranged on the floor.

The gradual decline of the overhead canopy opened the door to designs that emphasized headboards and footboards. In our collection of contemporary beds, these components—along with the color and figure of the wood itself—take center stage.

Beds, of course, are among the most standardized pieces of furniture in the house. They must be made to accommodate mattresses that only come in so many sizes. But working within these constraints still leaves room for inventive compositions.

Duo Bed

Bill Huston

The Duo Bed, says maker Bill Huston, gets its name from reversible head- and footboards, allowing either hammered copper or cherry panels to face outward.

Huston's furniture company, which employs four craftsmen, is located in Kennebunkport, Maine, and serves not only residential clients but also public libraries, colleges, corporations, and small businesses. Huston founded the firm in 1988 after working with Thomas Moser for 12 years.

"Subtle understatement has been a goal," he writes, "adding simple inlays that develop the design but don't dominate, using a soft curve to lighten a severe, hard line, and letting the grain and color of the wood emerge as a design element."

Huston says a variety of furniture traditions have influenced his work, including Scandinavian, Shaker, Arts and Crafts, and Asian. "Rather than simply take these styles and mimic or reproduce them, I have felt them and then interpreted and evolved my own designs," he says.

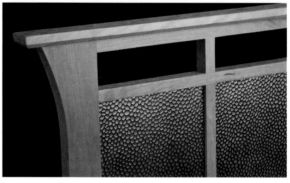

Size: 71 in. deep, 84 in. wide, 48 in. tall

Materials: American black cherry, hammered copper

Finish: Watco® oil with satin conversion varnish

Contact: www.hustonandcompany.com

Bill Huston's Duo bed features a reversible headboard and sturdy steel hardware that ensures a secure connection between the side rails and the legs.

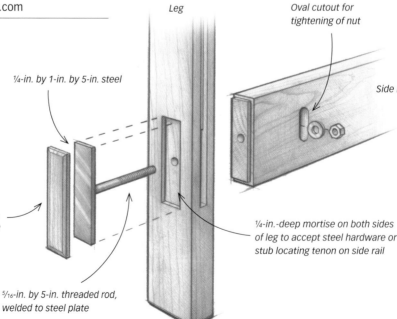

Leg

Oval cutout for tightening of nut

¼-in. by 1-in. by 5-in. steel

Side rail

¼-in. by 5¼-in. wood, epoxied to steel plate

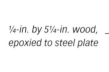

⁵⁄₁₆-in. by 5-in. threaded rod, welded to steel plate

¼-in.-deep mortise on both sides of leg to accept steel hardware or stub locating tenon on side rail

Sun Comes Up Bed

Hugh Montgomery

Hugh Montgomery was asked to design this bed for an east-facing bedroom in coastal Camden, Maine, with a view of Penobscot Bay. That was not long after he had visited Greene and Greene's Gamble House on the opposite side of the country, and the result was a mix of influences.

"The simplistic beauty of the Gamble House screen door captured my attention enough that I took a photograph of the door," Montgomery says. "Soon thereafter, when I got this commission, it seemed natural to create a design based on this Craftsman-style sunray motif that I was taken with."

Montgomery says his furniture should succeed on more than one level, not only with its overall design but also in the details. The wavy figure of the veneer, for instance, suggests the rippling of water.

Montgomery is a Maine native who now works on Bainbridge Island in Washington, a ferry ride from Seattle. Among his important work habits is a coffee break at 10 sharp. "You can't beat freshly roasted coffee," he says. "I find several cups of good coffee really keep the work flowing."

Size: 78 in. deep, 57 in. wide, 47 in. tall

Materials: Solid cherry, resawn cherry veneer, holly

Finish: Oil-varnish mix

Contact: www.hughmontgomery.com

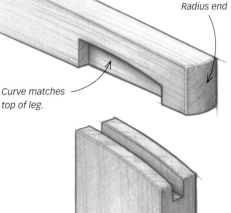

Radius end

Curve matches top of leg.

Leg is proud of top rail approximately ⅛ in. on both sides.

Hugh Montgomery devised this bridle joint to connect the legs of the Sun Comes Up Bed with the top rail of the headboard.

Mystic Bed

William Doub

"This bed represents the current evolution of my own style, which I term 'Nouveau Rustique,'" says New Hampshire furniture maker William Doub. "It is an original synthesis of Art-Nouveau-inspired lines with rustic decorative elements derived from nature."

A full-time maker since 1973, Doub says the biggest design challenge was coming up with an asymmetrical shape for the queen-size bed whose lines didn't compete with each other, "and knowing when to stop." From a construction standpoint, carving the feet proved the most difficult part of the project.

Doub made a number of conceptual drawings, which helped him come to a final design with his clients, and then a set of full-scale shop drawings. But there was no prototype.

Doub studied furniture making at the North Bennet Street School in Boston and is drawn to the work of a diverse group of artists that includes Émile Gallé, Émile-Jacques Ruhlmann, George Nakashima, Sam Maloof, and Wharton Esherick.

And if he were to make the piece again? "I would make it a king-size bed," he says. (See p. 80 for Doub's Tamworth Chair.)

Size: Headboard up to 72 in., footboard to 42 in.

Materials: Black walnut, curly cherry veneer, decorative elements from various exotic woods

Finish: Marine-grade varnish

Contact: www.customfurniture-doub.com

SEATING

We interact with chairs in a way unlike any other type of furniture. If a table or cabinet is poorly designed, it is easy to look the other way. But we may use a dining chair for two or three hours at a stretch, an office chair for an entire day. There is no ignoring an unsuccessful design when it leads to physical discomfort.

Chairs also must survive occasionally tough circumstances: users who fidget and shift their weight from side to side, push themselves across the floor, or even tilt back on two legs.

These requirements are above and beyond any design goals the maker might have, and possibly for these reasons some furniture makers never get around to making chairs, benches, and other kinds of seating. We were surprised to see so many submissions, and these 26 contemporary and interpretative designs prove that seating is far from an overlooked niche.

Cord Chair

Jeff O'Brien

Oregon furniture maker Jeff O'Brien was looking for something "really comfortable" when he started work on this dining room side chair for himself and his wife. A class taught by chairmaker Brian Boggs, as well as a chair made by Garrett Hack, got him pointed in the right direction.

It was O'Brien's first attempt at designing a chair, although he's promised to make six more in cherry. He found the compound angles in the upper part of the back were probably the most difficult part of construction and adds: "As in all chairs, it's not the positive space but the negative that seems to take on more importance."

Working with Danish cord also was something new. O'Brien's wife had grown up in a house with chairs that incorporated it and had suggested he use it here. He found the weave wasn't that difficult, but working with the material was tough on his fingers.

O'Brien lives in West Linn, Ore., on the banks of the Willamette River. "My shop is nothing special," he says, "just a converted garage. I guess it's the location that makes it special." (O'Brien's nightstand appears on p. 25.)

Size: 20 in. deep, 17¼ in. wide, 34½ in. tall

Materials: Santos mahogany, steam-bent ash, Danish cord

Finish: Oil-varnish mix

Contact: www.dogwood-design.com

Linnea Bar Stool

John Thoe

Looking for a way to expand his line of dining furniture, Seattle furniture maker John Thoe set out to design a comfortable bar stool that would stand on its own merits as a sculptural piece.

The end result seems graceful and natural, but it reflects a complex design effort to extend the use of arcs and ellipses in his dining chairs. "The negative spaces above the seat relate almost as mirror shapes but not in size to the negatives spaces below the seat," Thoe writes. "These negative spaces are quadrilateral polygons, two parallel lines joined by two unparallel lines."

Thoe, who has been making furniture for 25 years, apprenticed for two years to a master acanthus carver in Norway. Then, 15 years ago, he bought two upholstered dining chair designs from Michael Strong. Thoe now maintains two businesses: traditional carved furniture and a line of dining furniture.

He has worked by himself for the last nine years. "At age 55, I realize tabletops will be difficult to handle when I am in my 80s," he says. "Perhaps then I will need to hire another employee."

Size: 21 in. deep, 23 in. wide, 44 in. tall

Materials: Cherry

Finish: Conversion lacquer

Contact: www.johnthoe.com

Claro Walnut Chair

Curtis Minier

The design for this chair had its origins in a large dining table that Curtis Minier was asked to make. The table could expand from 9 ft. to 12 ft. long and Minier's clients had specified there was to be no visible support beneath its claro-walnut top.

Minier's solution was to conceal a steel bracket connecting the table's legs and the bubinga rails. When it came to a chair design, Minier borrowed the idea of incorporating steel.

"My work habits include making detailed drawings, planning the steps to build the pieces before the beginning, and working consistent hours at a steady pace during weekdays," says Minier, a furniture maker for 32 years. "This allows me to turn out a lot of work during the week so that I have time for other activities I enjoy."

He works alone in a 1,200-sq.-ft. shop, which he designed and built, along with his house, on Vashon Island, Wash. (Curtis Minier's blanket chest appears on p. 116.)

Size: 20 in. deep, 24 in. wide, 30½ in. tall

Materials: Claro walnut, bubinga, brass-coated steel

Finish: Lacquer

Contact: curtminier@gmail.com

Curtis Minier's armchair incorporates a framework of steel, an idea that grew out of an earlier commission for a large dining table. The brass-coated steel has a dark patina that helps it blend with the chair's claro-walnut legs and bubinga back.

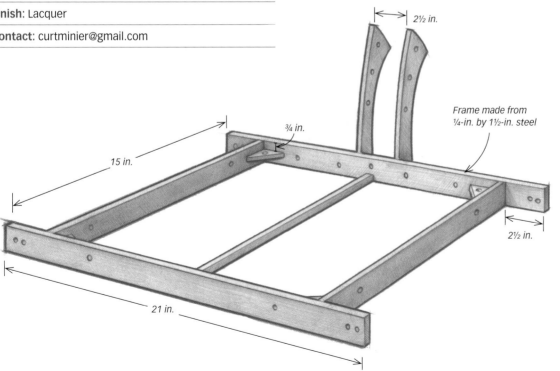

2½ in.

¾ in.

15 in.

Frame made from ¼-in. by 1½-in. steel

2½ in.

21 in.

Slate Bench

Craig Thibodeau

San Diego, Calif., furniture maker Craig Thibodeau was commissioned to make this bench for clients who wanted it to match the style, color, and veneer of the bed and nightstands they already owned. That might have been challenge enough, but they also wanted a bench that was light enough to move around the room easily.

Thibodeau's solution was to make the seat as a torsion box with an ultralight plywood core. End panels and the lower shelf are made with the same plywood and skinned with ⅛-in. medium-density fiberboard to provide a smooth foundation for the veneer.

Veneering curved surfaces proved to be one of the more difficult parts of the project. Although Thibodeau did not build a full prototype, he did make some trial runs with veneer to work the kinks out of the process. He says he would look for ways to simplify it further if he were to build the bench again.

Thibodeau, a fan of both Émile-Jacques Ruhlmann and James Krenov, works in a 1,000-sq.-ft. space not far from home. He has been making furniture professionally for eight years and now tends toward more difficult, curved designs. "This seems to be a phase many craftspeople go through, trying to prove to themselves or others that they have the requisite technical skills to do the work required. I have not satisfied myself that I do yet."

Size: 16 in. deep, 54 in. wide, 18 in. tall

Materials: Myrtle burl and maple veneer, medium-density fiberboard, ultralight plywood, silk

Finish: Polished polyester, black pigmented lacquer

Contact: www.ctfinefurniture.com

Upholstered Settee

Timothy Coleman

This graceful and relatively simple settee might come as a surprise to those who have seen some of Timothy Coleman's intricately detailed cabinets. But the settee is right at home in Coleman's wide-ranging design repertoire.

"My style and preferences haven't changed so much as they have continued to bounce back and forth between designs that are straightforward and utilitarian and more sculptural," Coleman writes. "In both cases, however, I am striving for well-balanced and proportioned forms and a thoughtful use of materials." (For a pair of side tables by Coleman, see p. 17.)

The settee emerged from a commissioned piece that Coleman had done a few years earlier. In addition to changing some of the proportions in the original, Coleman replaced a wooden seat with this upholstered version. As is the case with any type of seating, he says, the trick is producing something that looks good from a number of angles.

Coleman started with concept sketches that focused on the parts that make up the back. Full-size drawings and then a full-scale mock-up followed to help him fine-tune the angle between back and seat.

"I'm sure if I were to approach it again I would make further refinements," he says. "They would be small changes this time, mostly with regard to the way certain parts converge. I think the piece is fine as it is, but any re-design gives an opportunity to try something different."

Size: 19 in. deep, 43 in. wide, 33 in. tall

Materials: Jatoba, silk

Finish: Tung oil-urethane mix

Contact: www.timothycoleman.com

Cantata Chair

Jeff Miller

Although some furniture makers work from drawings or even rough sketches, Chicago's Jeff Miller falls solidly in the prototype camp. "The defining moment when working on the design for this chair was when I put together a cardboard prototype," he says. "Once I saw that—crude as it was—I knew I had what I was looking for."

The design borrows elements from chairs that Miller had built in the past, although he says it's very different from much of his previous work. Miller says the joinery was a challenge, although not as difficult as the double-tapered laminations that make up the back legs.

Miller also teaches and writes about furniture making. His shop, where he also conducts classes, is a 3,000-sq.-ft. former post office just blocks from home.

"I work a normal 9-to-5 business week and then teach most Saturdays throughout the year," he says. "Although I often can't hear it with machines running, I usually have classical music playing while I work."

Size: 21 in. deep, 20 in. wide, 39 in. tall

Materials: Walnut (left) or mahogany (right), leather

Finish: Custom oil-varnish blend

Contact: www.furnituremaking.com

Folding Bar Stool

Katrina Tompkins

Katrina Tompkins works only with locally harvested wood, offcuts, and scraps, the kinds of material that will have the least possible effect on the environment. "Functionality is equally important," she says, "because if not, then it's also a waste of materials. Most things I make have a second function."

Those twin objectives are at work here. This bar stool is made from locally salvaged black locust and walnut scrap from other projects, and it can be used as a short, folding ladder or a place to sit. An internal hinge that joins the legs and allows the stool to be folded up and tucked away was Tompkins' biggest technical challenge.

Tompkins is a second-year student at Canada's Sheridan College, where she takes advantage of the school's studio space. Otherwise, she sets up in either her bedroom or the backyard. "I am a chronic list maker," she says. "I love to keep organized and cross it off the list."

Size: 24 in. deep, 16¾ in. wide, 43 in. tall

Materials: Black locust, black walnut dowel, brass

Finish: Hemp oil

Contact: www.katrinatompkins.com

A hinge plate made from ½-in. plywood allows the legs of Katrina Tompkins' folding bar stool to open and close. The plate is pinned firmly in place on the longer leg and pivots on the other.

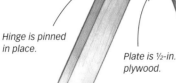

1 in. by 2½ in.

Open

Folded

Hinge is pinned in place.

Plate is ½-in. plywood.

Mendo Bench

Greg Klassen

Greg Klassen got the idea for this bench on a visit to the Pacific Ocean, where he stopped to admire the waves and contemplate the beach environment. "I wanted to bring this feeling of life into my design for this bench," he says. "There are no square or flat surfaces on the bench, just as there are no such things in nature."

Klassen, a second-year student at College of the Redwoods in northern California, coopered the madrone seat from three pieces, roughing out the shape on a tablesaw by repeatedly adjusting the fence and blade height. He smoothed the contours with two planes he made and says the seamless flow of wood makes even other woodworkers wonder how it was done.

Klassen has been making furniture for only a few years. He was headed for a life as a pastoral minister after graduating with a biblical studies degree. Poor and newly married, he needed furniture. "I was working at a door factory at the time and decided to make my own furniture from door parts," he says. "I loved it. Soon I realized making furniture was what I was supposed to be doing with my life."

Size: 20 in. deep, 36 in. wide, 18 in. deep

Materials: Madrone, claro walnut

Finish: Oil-varnish mix, wax

Contact: www.gregklassen.com

Walton NE (New Edition) Chair

Peter Thompson

Maine furniture maker Peter Thompson says he began his building career with small cabinets whose curved sides and stained-glass panels strayed from traditional lines. But, he adds, "My interest in cabinets has been placed on the back burner as I have found an incredible love for designing and building chairs and stools."

The Walton NE chair is the third iteration in a series, this one with a backboard that bows inward toward the front of the chair. Thompson says the new design is not only stronger than the original, but also is more comfortable because of better lower-back support.

"One of my main goals was to design a chair that had movement and connective flow," he says. "The curve of the front legs is mimicked to a certain degree in the curve below the seat of the back legs. One is a compound curve of the other."

Thompson, who works in a 26-ft. by 34-ft. shop he built near his home in Cornville, says he's inspired by Sam Maloof and Tony Kenway. But he draws on the work of a large group of furniture makers "when it comes to breaking down visually what I think works and doesn't work."

Size: 22 in. deep, 20 in. wide, 33¾ in. tall

Materials: Black walnut, oak

Finish: Linseed oil and wax

Contact: www.peterthompsonfurniture.com

Low Chair

Eric Connor

Eric Connor designed and built this chair for an exhibition sponsored by the Crafts Council of Ireland. The County Dublin furniture maker was asked to draw on 19th-century Irish designs and to use traditional techniques in creating a piece that would seem at home in a contemporary setting.

Connor, a self-taught professional who has been making furniture for 15 years and now specializes in chairs, steam-bent the curved members and used through-wedged joints at the seat. Boring the angled holes in the 1-in. by 1-in. back proved to be one of the more difficult technical parts of the design.

"Simplicity and elegance have always been my goals," Connor writes. "I've drawn from the influence of the traditional and have kept progressing, following my heart and instincts rather than trends or fashion."

He says one improvement would be to use laminated arm supports rather than steam-bent parts to eliminate springback and gain greater consistency.

Size: 16 in. deep, 20 in. wide, 29 in. tall

Materials: Ash, tulipwood

Finish: Lacquer

Contact: www.thecraftdirectory.ie/ericconnor

East Chair
Jari-Pekka Vilkman

A gonizing over a design is par for the course for many furniture makers, so the satisfaction is all the sweeter when the result is exactly as intended. "I definitely hope I have a chance to make more of these chairs," says Finland's Jari-Pekka Vilkman. "It's a damn good chair."

His intent was simply to build a comfortable and modern chair that showed some Chinese influence. If the finished work looks effortless and simple, consider that it took five or six mock-ups before Vilkman thought he had the design right.

Vilkman's work shows a wide range of styles, from these pleasingly spare side chairs to his sculptural Coastline series (see his Monolith sofa table on p. 8 and a lowboard on p. 142). Although he tries not to look to other furniture makers for inspiration, he admits, "E.J. Ruhlmann was the man."

"As I am Scandinavian," he says, "I got simplicity in my mother's milk and my pieces are starting to get more minimalistic. Still, I want to load my pieces with details. My work is starting to be more sculptural and free-form and that's the way I will push in the future."

Size: 24 in. deep, 21 in. wide, 34 in. tall

Materials: Wenge, ash, oak

Finish: Lacquer

Contact: www.j-pvilkman.com

SEATING

Size: 17 in. deep, 57 in. wide, 20 in. tall

Materials: Dyed mahogany, leather

Finish: Nitrocellulose lacquer

Contact: www.greentreehome.com

Lady Edith's Bench
Don Green

Some furniture makers will produce a piece only once, epitomizing what "one-off" furniture is all about. But Don Green has looked for ways to streamline construction as he makes multiple copies, keeping his furniture affordable and marketable.

Lady Edith's Bench is part of a collection (also see Miss Olivia's Writing Desk on pp. 96-97) that fulfills Green's objective of producing "strong, honest work that is both functional and sound in construction."

Keeping a careful eye on the market has helped shape Green's approach to furniture making. "I decided to build and offer the pieces in materials that were readily available," he writes, "like mahogany, sapele, cherry, dyed and stained woods, and standard leather colors."

It's an approach rooted in practicality. Customers who see his work online or in a magazine expect to see the same thing when they place an order. That said, Green is happy to oblige a customer whose tastes run to the more exotic.

Looking for efficiencies also has affected Green's view of the construction process. "When I set out to make the first set of samples, I invested time in documenting the measurements as well as building jigs and fixtures for all the pieces," Green says.

Green works by himself in a 3,000-sq.-ft. shop in Delhi, N.Y., in the foothills of the Catskill Mountains. His wife, Jenifer, is his business partner and handles sales. After 20 years making furniture, he finds he works a regular five-day week, at least most of the time. Making efficiency a priority has had that benefit, too.

Kathy's Chair

Scott King

While a student at the Inside Passage School of Fine Woodworking, Scott King needed a project and opted for a chair—his first. He started with elements he liked in chairs by two other furniture makers, Garrett Hack and Ejler Hjorth-Westh, and went forward from there.

King thought the Danish cord he chose for the seat would help the chair feel somewhat informal, but weaving the pattern was anything but simple. To prevent the cord from exerting unequal pressure on the chair's rails, King ended up weaving both top and bottom. That added time and complexity to the project, but King says the detail gives considerable strength to the frame.

King built a mock-up of the chair from poplar, allowing him to play with different leg and rail shapes. That also gave him a chance to sketch some ideas for the back on cardboard and clamp them in place to see how they'd look.

Compound-angled joinery proved a major challenge. "There are a lot of factors to keep synchronized at the same time," he says. "If you forget about one for a short time, things can get out of alignment very quickly." (King's treasure box appears on pp. 150-151.)

Size: 18 in. deep, 20 in. wide, 36 in. tall

Materials: Yellow narra, Danish cord

Finish: Oil-varnish mix

Contact: www.scottkingfurniture.com

Embrace Bench

Peter Chen

At the start of Peter Chen's woodworking career, he bought the books of James Krenov and thought about emulating his approach to furniture making. But as time went on, Chen found himself drawn to a more modernist style. "I still very much admire and appreciate fine handcrafted furniture," Chen writes, "but it's something that I have very little desire to do myself."

In fact, Chen's plywood bench began with a piece of manufactured furniture, the Nelson platform bench made by Herman Miller from slats of maple. In designing his own version, Chen moved the legs all the way out to the ends for better stability. And he built the whole thing from plywood ripped into strips and edge-glued to form broad planks.

The bench was originally designed to consume a single 4-ft. by 8-ft. sheet of plywood, with the only waste created by the sawkerfs. The legs are connected to the benchtop with two aluminum rods at each end. "Every detail is visible and to me this is the embodiment of structural honesty," Chen says.

Chen describes himself as a part-time professional who pursues furniture making on weekends and in the evening in a cooperative shop he helped start in East Vancouver, Canada. Chen works almost exclusively with engineered materials, and says all designs and cut lists are done on a computer using AutoCAD.

Size: 19 in. deep, 60 in. wide, 16½ in. tall

Materials: Plywood, aluminum rods

Finish: Lacquer

Contact: www.casikamodern.com

Velda's Writing-Arm Chair

Curtis Buchanan

Curtis Buchanan makes three kinds of writing-arm Windsors, a traditional style that combines a seat with a portable desk. The form dates to the first part of the 18th century and early examples can be formal, even imposing, in their proportions.

With this one, Buchanan wanted a more contemporary feeling and the seat proved to be the sticking point. "Designing a seat to match the style of the rest of the chair was a challenge," he says. The first glimmer of a solution came from a dusty Thomas Moser catalog Buchanan found in the loft of his shop.

Almost all of Buchanan's traditional Windsors are painted, but this version takes full advantage of stunning walnut sawn by the same man who eventually took possession of the chair.

Unlike many professional furniture makers, Buchanan uses neither sketches ("I can't draw") nor prototypes to develop new chair styles. "I design in a way that is not very smart," he says. "I build the chair, making it up as I go along. It works most of the time."

The self-taught Buchanan uses mostly hand tools in his 16-ft. by 20-ft. timber-frame shop in the backyard of his Jonesborough, Tenn., home. "The neighborhood kids like to stop in and visit," he says. "That's nice."

Size: 30 in. deep, 30 in. wide, 46 in. tall

Materials: Walnut, white oak

Finish: Penetrating oil

Contact: www.curtisbuchananchairmaker.com

Tamworth Chair

William Doub

The design for this chair grew out of a decorative element on an altar podium that had been commissioned by a group of Unitarian-Universalists for a new church sanctuary. Repeated in the chair back, says maker William Doub, the motif represents the pastor holding up her hands and tying together the threads of various religions, an underlying tenet of the faith.

Doub met with a church committee a number of times as the design took shape and managed to work within the confines of a church budget, the biggest challenge of the project.

He went on to make this chair again, substituting walnut for the chair seat because it is easier to carve than the original cherry.

With a 15,000-sq.-ft. shop (about a third of a former air-compressor factory), Doub now works with a number of younger partners. "At this point in my career, instruction and mentoring are as much a priority as the actual design and fabrication of my work," he says. (Doub's Mystic Bed appears on p. 57.)

Size: 21 in. deep, 20 in. wide, 38 in. tall

Materials: Cherry

Finish: Marine-grade varnish

Contact: www.customfurniture-doub.com

Hall Bench

James Hoyne

James Hoyne made this hall bench as a class project at the Northwest Woodworking Studio in Portland, Ore.

Starting with a complete set of *Fine Woodworking* back issues, Hoyne read everything he could find on benches before starting to sketch a design for his own. Full-scale drawings plus a prototype made from cardboard helped him check overall proportions.

Hoyne says he admires the work of many early Arts and Crafts furniture makers, particularly Edward Barnsley, and has been slowly adding curves to his work as he develops his own style.

Hoyne, who lives in Big Sky, Mont., has been making furniture for five years. "I work in a single-car garage, 10 ft. by 20 ft.," he says. "Everything is on rollers and large pieces are a challenge. I live in the mountains at 5,500 ft. We have snow from October to May, so it makes working in the driveway a challenge."

Size: 17 in. deep, 48 in. wide, 19⅛ in. tall

Materials: Ash, ebony

Finish: Shellac, polyurethane, wax

Contact: www.bigskycustomfurniture.com

Drove

Jennifer Anderson

Jennifer Anderson's series of chairs, called Drove, started with an observation she made after completing a commissioned set of dining chairs. Gathered together without a table, the chairs looked like a group of animals or people and she thought that exploring this "anthropomorphic quality" further could be interesting.

"Drove is a metaphor for people," she says. "Just as humans are made up of pretty much the same parts, the individual chairs also share the same building blocks. But just as humans are very different from each other, the chairs in Drove are far from the sum of their parts."

Each chair has a different height, width, and seat angle. Anderson points out that the differences between the tallest and shortest chairs are obvious, but it is harder to spot differences in seat angle. "The subtlety in these differences allowed me to explore ergonomics," she says.

Anderson likes to mix traditional and unconventional materials, which in this case means combining walnut with polyethylene wrapped in industrial felt. Tenons that connect the side stretchers with the legs are pinned with polypropylene rods. (For Anderson's hanging room divider, see p. 149).

Size: Seat heights vary from 13 in. to 21 in. Chair in photo at right is 20 in. deep, 20 in. wide, 21 in. tall

Materials: Walnut, polyethylene, industrial felt

Finish: Hand-rubbed oil

Contact: www.jenniferandersonstudio.com

Cherry Dining Chair

Craig Jentz

A tall-backed Italian chair that Craig Jentz and his wife had admired became the design foundation for a set of their own. But their collaboration extended beyond choosing a style: Jentz found his wife's work as a physical therapist specializing in back problems a big help in making the chairs ergonomically correct.

Jentz worked through a number of prototypes to perfect the curves and dimensions of the chair back and pronounces the end result "extremely comfortable."

From a construction standpoint, the curved and tapered back proved a major challenge. It is made from five plies of solid wood, the outer two of uniform thickness and the inner three tapered.

"I used a friend's large but out-of-tune bandsaw," says Jentz, a longtime amateur furniture maker in Minneapolis. "As there are 12 chairs, we went through a lot of lumber, lots of blades, and lots of sawdust."

Size: 22 in. deep, 27 in. wide, 52 in. tall

Materials: Cherry, leather

Finish: Oil

Slate Bench

Mark Sfirri

This bench gets its name from the stone it resembles, but it's actually made from painted mahogany. The unusual undercarriage is assembled from lathe-turned parts that also have been carved.

"I like to experiment with forms generated on the lathe," says New Hope, Pa., furniture maker Mark Sfirri. "The detail in the leg was an experiment that I thought could work as a central carved detail in this work."

Sfirri says he generally likes to include turned parts in his work and in the early 1990s began experimenting with multi-axis turning, a technique that can produce sculptural, asymmetrical shapes.

The most difficult part of this bench, Sfirri says, was the seat, which is angled identically on top and bottom. "It made for some tricky calculations to have it sit

properly," he says. Sfirri worked from sketches, full-size drawings, and a mock-up of the end of the bench.

Sfirri, a furniture maker since 1972, studied under Tage Frid at the Rhode Island School of Design and now works in a 900-sq.-ft. shop that was once a dog kennel. New Hope is fertile ground: It's the same town where the Nakashima workshops are located and not that far from Paoli, home to Wharton Esherick, one of Sfirri's favorite artists.

Size: 20 in. deep, 71 in. wide, 17½ in. tall

Materials: Mahogany

Finish: Paint

Contact: marksfirri@gmail.com

Entryway Bench
Aspy Khambatta

Aspy Khambatta's entryway bench was a commission from someone who had seen his jewelry boxes in a New York gallery. "It is not obvious," Khambatta writes, "but the design evolved from the armrests down."

Key to construction is a 7-ft. turning that supports the front legs, seat slats, and armrests. Khambatta says a turning of that size was challenging enough, but it also had to come apart so he could create a flat surface for the seat slats and a recess for the armrests and front leg assemblies.

Khambatta, a mostly self-taught professional, works in a 7,500-sq.-ft. cooperative shop he helped launch 35 years ago in Berkeley, Calif. What started as "an incubator for self-guided artists and craftsmen" is now home to 10 woodworkers and two painters.

"I cannot say that I have been influenced by a particular furniture maker, although I admire several," he says. "As a designer you observe everything around you in detail and in overview, you digest the information, and eventually it expresses itself in your work."

Size: 26 in. deep, 84 in. wide, 18 in. tall

Materials: Maple, wenge, bronze

Finish: Oil and wax

Contact: aspy-judy@comcast.net

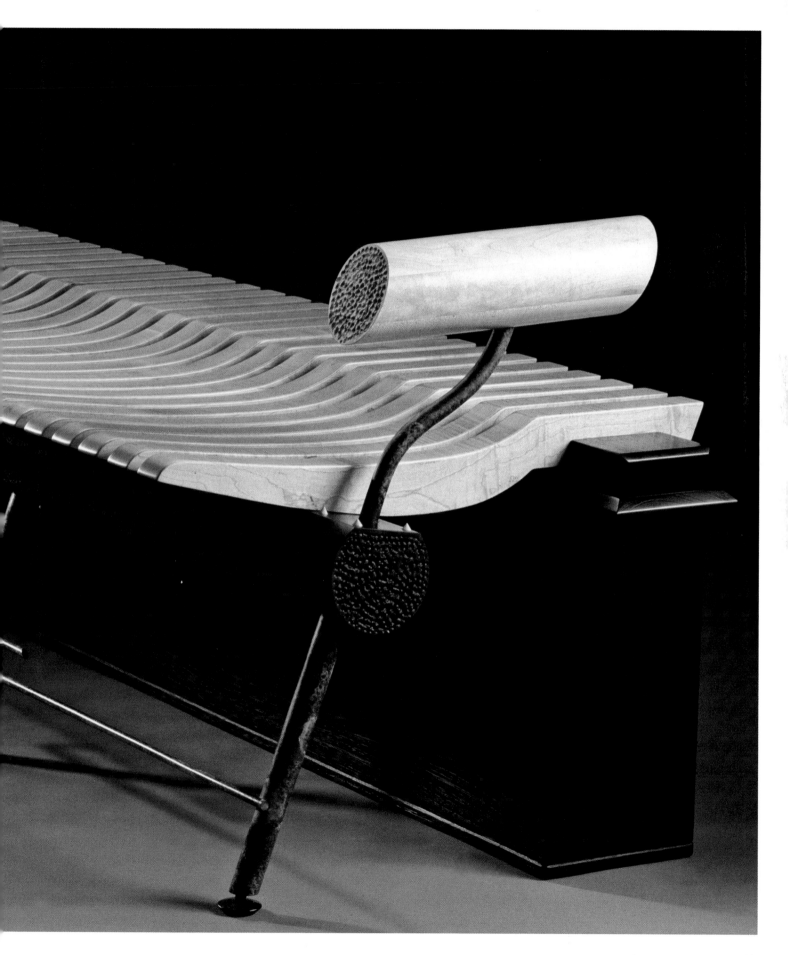

Pearwood
Dining Chairs

Loy Martin

There were both stylistic and practical challenges for Loy Martin in the design of these dining chairs. On the aesthetic side, the chairs had to be compatible with both a Georgian drop-leaf table in dark mahogany and a contemporary table made of pearwood and bubinga. From a practical standpoint, the chairs had to be comfortable over an extended period of time.

"The idea was to make comfortable dining chairs that would mediate stylistically between the contemporary studio pieces and the 17th- and 18th-century antiques already in the room," says Martin, a 25-year professional in Palo Alto, Calif.

He took a design clue from three small Windsor chairs in the room, translating an ovoid detail set below their crest rails into the rosewood inlays in the new chairs.

As to comfort, Martin drew on his experience. "I've learned that larger people can be more comfortable in a smaller chair than smaller people can be in a larger chair," Martin says. "So, I tend to make my dining chairs a bit smaller than standard, especially in seat height. I always include lumbar support in the seat backs."

Size: 22 in. deep, 19 in. wide, 34½ in. tall

Materials: Pearwood, Brazilian rosewood, fabric

Finish: Lacquer

Contact: loym@batnet.com

Ash Chair

Nate Blaisdell

Nate Blaisdell's focus was comfort as well as aesthetics when he designed this gracefully curved chair in ash. "There was a lot of focus on comfort," he writes, "as I wanted a chair that could be formal yet comfortable for hours."

Blaisdell, a graduate of the Rochester Institute of Technology, started with small sketches, then built a scale model, and finally produced full working drawings. He says the idea of incorporating spaces in the front and back legs developed as he made a number of small models.

"I usually build a quick mock-up to address any issues such as proportions and balance," he says. "Usually this is out of cardboard or another quick working material that best suits the situation."

Technically, Blaisdell found the double-tapered laminations, his first, challenging, as was making sure the reverse-curve back was as comfortable as he had hoped. Were he to make the chair again, Blaisdell says he would look for ways to lighten up the front and side rails. (A cabinet by Blaisdell appears on pp. 138-139.)

Size: 22 in. deep, 17 in. wide, 44 in. tall

Materials: Ash, micro suede

Finish: Polyacrylic, milk paint

Contact: blaisdelldesign@gmail.com

Arrow Armchair

Peter Turner

Peter Turner's armchair gets its name from the shape of the armrests, which remind him of the feathers that guide the trajectory of an arrow. But the chair really developed around the shape of the leg, which Turner likes so much he plans to use it in a full line of furniture.

Turner sketched the leg during a lull at a craft show. He originally envisioned it as part of a headboard for a bed, but later incorporated it into this spec-built chair. He built a prototype of poplar, ⅛-in. bending plywood, and cardboard to make sure the chair would be comfortable and to check dimensions and proportions.

He chose a Danish-cord seat for its texture and protected it with blond shellac. (See Turner's hutch on p. 124.)

Turner is a self-taught furniture maker who says he's "learned a ton" over the last eight years by teaching at the Center for Furniture Craftsmanship in Rockport, Maine. He works in a 23-ft. by 27-ft. two-car garage in South Portland, Maine, with "a bunch of old machines and plenty of windows."

The shop overlooks city-owned woods and a small brook. "After big rains," he says, "I have a water view."

Size: 17½ in. deep, 23 in. wide, 32½ in. tall

Materials: Riftsawn white oak, Danish cord

Finish: Mix of varnish, tung oil, and citrus thinner

Contact: www.petersturner.com

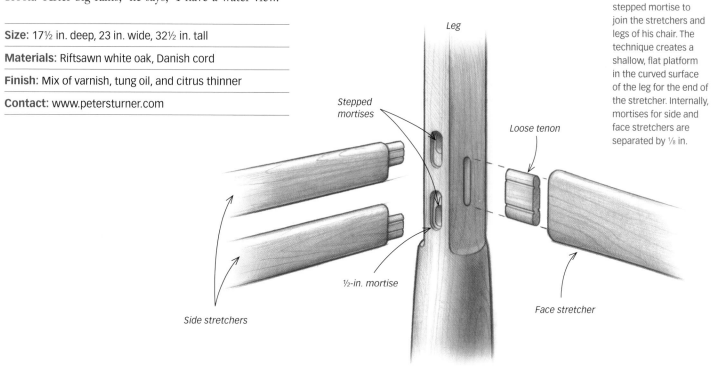

Peter Turner used a stepped mortise to join the stretchers and legs of his chair. The technique creates a shallow, flat platform in the curved surface of the leg for the end of the stretcher. Internally, mortises for side and face stretchers are separated by ⅛ in.

Leg

Stepped mortises

Loose tenon

½-in. mortise

Side stretchers

Face stretcher

Plywood Chair
Ryan McNew

Ryan McNew's design process is more about thinking on your feet than planning in advance. "Encountering challenges and coming up with creative solutions are both part of the process and evolution that each piece goes through from start to finish," McNew says.

Designing this plywood chair was "short and mostly mental, with emphasis on allowing myself to be influenced by pre-existing organic and man-made objects," McNew says. "I always try to determine the form or shape of the object first, the function second, and lastly how the idea will be executed."

He used rough sketches but no prototype and says the biggest hurdle was gluing up oversize forms in a vacuum bag.

McNew has been making furniture for five years. He studied furniture design at Herron School of Art and Design and shares a 400-sq.-ft. shop with another furniture maker not far from home in Indianapolis.

Size: 25 in. deep, 22 in. wide, 30 in. tall

Materials: Ebonized plywood

Finish: Graphite, lacquer

Contact: www.ryanmcnewfurniture.com

Rocking Chair

Tony Kenway

Sam Maloof's influence seems obvious in this rocking chair by Australian furniture maker Tony Kenway, but he also took hints from a Shaker rocker he found comfortable and well balanced.

Kenway credits both Maloof and his mother, herself a woodworker and furniture maker, with inspiring his work (for more, see his desk and chair on p. 98). There also was the two years he worked as a boatbuilder early in his career, an experience that helped him visualize complex shapes in three dimensions. Much of his work, in fact, now incorporates sculptural shapes and compound curves.

The design of this chair has been evolving over the past 20 years. As he explained in a slide narrative with Jon Binzen for *Fine Woodworking* magazine, Kenway has pared down the thickness of the parts over time, refining its appearance and giving it more flexibility.

The chair is made from a local hardwood, quilted Tasmanian blackwood, all of it solid except for its bent-laminated rockers. Working in a shop with three employees, Kenway uses "extensive" full-size drawings and mock-ups to arrive at final designs.

Kenway is still tinkering with the designs for some of his furniture, but not the rocker. "This piece is resolved," he says, "and in limited production."

Size: 30 in. deep, 24 in. wide, 30 in. tall

Materials: Quilted Tasmanian blackwood

Finish: Oil and varnish

Contact: www.tonykenwayfurniture.com

DESKS

It's hard to make a practical case against the standard-issue office desks found in millions of American work cubicles. They provide a solid work surface and a place to stash paper, pens, and rubber bands. It's just that they aren't much to look at.

Yet take the same design requirements and put them in the hands of talented furniture makers, and look what happens. They prove that utility can coexist happily with beauty. Work surfaces can be something more than a bland sheet of plastic laminate made to look like granite. Why not something that looks like a carved leaf? There's no reason the supporting structure has to be plain and boxy when its curved form can flow like water.

Using any of these desks would be a reward in its own right, even if you had no more lofty a task than balancing the checkbook.

Miss Olivia's Writing Desk

Don Green

Don Green's educational background is in sculpture, not furniture making, and he points to versatile Art Deco designers Émile-Jacques Ruhlmann, André Groult, and Andre Arbus as especially important to his own work.

The influences seem especially evident in this writing desk, whose elegantly curved top opens to an inset writing surface made of leather. "My work is pared down to simple elements that are designed and executed well," Green writes. "Decoration has never been my thing … I am not trying to reinvent the wheel but to develop my own language of form while at the same time honoring tradition."

True enough, the desk is almost completely without ornamentation. Its power emanates as much from a deceptively simple shape as it does from the rich figure of the sapele and details like the bronze drawer pulls.

This desk is named after one of Don and Jenifer Green's daughters, as are other pieces in this collection. In fact, they have mined the family roster of names with some regularity, choosing Jenifer's mother, nephews, nieces, and close friends to provide titles for Green's furniture.

Green says the desk is part of a collection of furniture he designed as a standard line that could be made efficiently in multiples (also see Lady Edith's Bench on pp. 74-75). The challenge, he adds, was in creating a collection that shares a common design thread.

Size: 27 in. deep, 42 in. wide, 38 in. tall

Materials: Sapele, dyed mahogany, leather, bronze

Finish: Nitrocellulose lacquer

Contact: www.greentreehome.com

Desk and Chair

Tony Kenway

Australia's Tony Kenway used rough sketches, then scale drawings, full-scale drawings, and finally full-scale mock-ups to create this subtly curvaceous desk in Tasmanian blackwood.

"The desk was designed with ultimate comfort in mind, with a curved front edge together with slatted pedestal ends to let the user feel as though he is 'in' the workspace," Kenway writes.

The desk includes three deep drawers whose handles are carved into the sculpted drawer fronts. Kenway says his biggest challenge was visualizing the desk in three dimensions and building drawers with compound-miter dovetails. Prototypes constructed using pine, cardboard, paint, and other materials helped sort out the details.

With three employees, Kenway maintains a shop in the hills near Byron Bay, Australia, in the same part of New South Wales where he was born. He uses only Australian lumber in his work.

Kenway says there is plenty of hand shaping involved in his furniture, which often uses sinuous shapes over straight lines. "I always preferred curved work with flowing lines," he writes (for more, see Kenway's Rocking Chair on p. 93).

Would there be any changes in the desk if he were to build it again? Yes, he says. It would be "slightly more sculptural."

Size: 33 in. deep, 59 in. wide, 30 in. tall

Materials: Tasmanian blackwood, cowhide insert

Finish: Oil and varnish

Contact: www.tonykenwayfurniture.com

Vesture Desk

Curtis Erpelding

Happenstance, history, and rejection all had something to do with Curtis Erpelding's Vesture Desk and matching chair. As Erpelding explains, the design originally was one of two options for clients who had ordered a desk for their son's room. They settled on the other, leaving Erpelding to build this one another day.

The son already had a Biedermeier sleigh bed and Erpelding picked up on its curves in the head and footboards when he designed the desk. The design also was a chance for Erpelding to expand on a "unibody" theme he had used in a sofa table years before.

Erpelding had trouble finding exactly the veneer he wanted and says the pattern that resulted was not something he ordinarily would have done. It was, he says, controlled by the pattern he was able to buy: "It took me in a direction I hadn't anticipated, yet I don't regret."

Erpelding, a 30-year self-taught professional who lives and works in Port Orchard, Wash., says the small curves of the side drawers where they meet the central pencil drawer are especially pleasing to him, even though they were the most difficult technical detail of the design.

Nor was it easy to avoid flaws in the sprayed finish. "Patience, time, and a little luck prevailed," he says.

Size: 24 in. deep, 66 in. wide, 29 in. tall

Materials: Bending plywood, ash, olive, ash burl veneer

Finish: Conversion varnish, pre-catalyzed lacquer

Contact: www.nwfinewoodworking.com

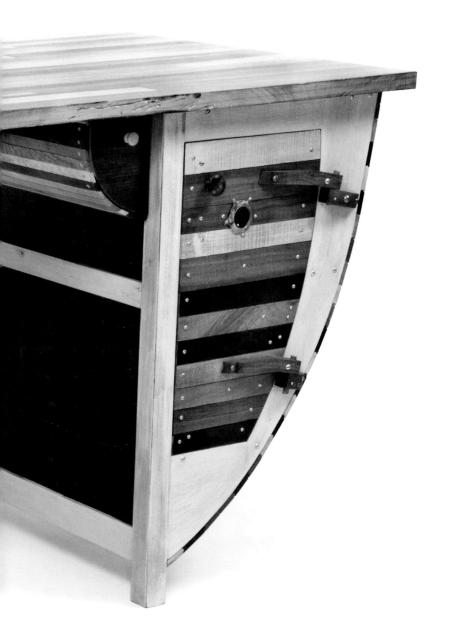

Captain Ronnie's Desk
Katie Hudnall

Katie Hudnall gets to her shop only after she's put in her 40 hours elsewhere. It's in an old outbuilding on a 300-acre farm where the owner often made do with what he had.

"Seeing the sorts of solutions that the old farmer came up with to keep this place running, and recognizing the ingenuity that comes from having a limited amount of time, tools, and materials has changed my idea of 'fine' woodworking," she writes. "The technical aspects of woodworking aren't really what interests me except for how they translate into the aesthetics of a piece."

She built this desk for a friend who spends as much time as he can on his boat, hence its curved, hull-like shape. And she used materials that otherwise would have ended up as kindling. It was all part of Hudnall's plan to build something that would suit Captain Ronnie's sensibilities while breaking away from conventional notions of what a desk should look like.

"I almost never build functional furniture," Hudnall says, "so designing something that would hold up to someone leaning or sitting on it without making it clunky was a challenge."

Size: 28 in. deep, 62 in. wide, 29 in. tall

Materials: Various wood scraps, medium-density fiberboard, glass lenses, copper, brass screws

Finish: Milk paint, wax, Waterlox

Contact: www.katiehudnall.com

Handel Leaf Desk #2

Mark Levin

Mark Levin's well-known Leaf series, a form he's been exploring for more than 20 years, poses challenges many woodworkers never have to face. Namely, how do you handle a blank for the top that weighs more than 450 lb. after it's been glued up yet must be moved constantly as it is whittled down to size?

Answer: An overhead hoist. It's one of many pieces of equipment in Levin's 2,500-sq.-ft. shop 25 miles east of Santa Fe, N.M., where he works alone. "After graduating college and suffering through that purity stage where everything had to be done by hand," Levin writes, "I'm now at the other end. If I can't do it with machinery or power tools, I don't do it. It's rather liberating, like never being constipated."

Levin studied woodworking at Northern Illinois University under Bobby Falwell, a graduate student of Wendell Castle, Levin's favorite furniture designer. Sculptors Constantin Brancusi and Isamu Noguchi also have left their marks.

The idea for this desk came from a collector who suggested it would make a good addition to Levin's ongoing Leaf series. He says he hesitated over concerns about scale and cost but has since gone on to make two. A third is in the works.

Size: 38 in. deep, 70 in. wide, 30 in. tall

Materials: Walnut

Finish: Deft® Danish oil

Contact: www.marklevin.com

Writing Desk

David Hurwitz

David Hurwitz's aim was to design a writing desk that was "completely asymmetrical and sculptural in form," without any square corners or right angles, and yet stable enough that its writing surface could be leaned on at any point along the edge.

With that in mind, Hurwitz paid careful attention to the geometry of the sculpted, tusk-like legs, building a scale model after he had worked out the design on paper. To keep the 1¾-in.-thick writing surface flat without benefit of aprons, breadboard ends, or battens, Hurwitz embedded ¾-in.-dia. steel rods in the edges of boards as he glued them up. The waxed rods, spaced about 18 in. apart, float in elongated holes to allow the wood to move seasonally.

Many of the names on Hurwitz's list of influential designers and furniture makers are familiar, the likes of Wharton Esherick and Charles Rennie Mackintosh. But Hurwitz also has embraced the work of architects and designers Carlo Mollino and Hector Guimard, sculptors Isamu Noguchi and Alexander Calder, surrealist painter Yves Tanguy, and even Dr. Seuss.

"My style has always been contemporary," he says, "but a warm contemporary that is organic, sensual, and inviting touch, not cold and forbidding like some contemporary furniture."

Size: 43 in. deep, 81 in. wide, 29 in. tall

Materials: Walnut, ash, steel

Finish: Top, Watco Danish Oil; legs, Bartley's® Gel Varnish

Contact: www.davidhurwitzoriginals.com

To make sure the top of this writing desk would stay flat, David Hurwitz concealed steel rods inside. Hurwitz bored holes for the ¾-in. rods in the planks used to make the top and waxed the steel so the wood could move seasonally.

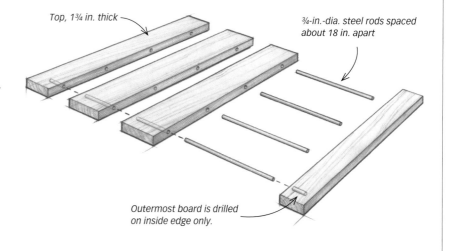

Top, 1¾ in. thick

¾-in.-dia. steel rods spaced about 18 in. apart

Outermost board is drilled on inside edge only.

CASE GOODS

The term "case goods" covers a lot of ground, spanning everything from bookcases and cabinets to chests and, increasingly, computer stations and audio cabinets.

We need these basic building blocks of furniture in every room of the house. At their simplest, case pieces may be little more than wooden boxes with an open face or a pair of doors. But they can be so much more than utilitarian storage bins for books, dishes, and clothes.

Classic forms such as breakfront chests, highboys, and towering Newport secretaries are still being faithfully reproduced in American shops. We looked for more contemporary interpretations and found imaginative uses of space and materials that could be just as commanding as early American masterpieces.

Whether they are made from solid wood or veneer over modern composites or honeycomb, case pieces are an opportunity for innovation in construction as well as design.

Wedding Chest
Miguel Gómez-Ibáñez

For Miguel Gómez-Ibáñez, a wedding chest built for his eldest son and his bride was a reminder that spontaneity can be a vital element of design.

Passing the time in a less-than-riveting lecture, Gómez-Ibáñez doodled the original design for this chest on a napkin. Later, when he translated the sketch into more formal drawings, he realized the life had gone

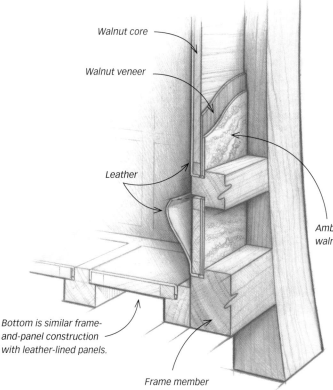

Walnut core

Walnut veneer

Leather

Bottom is similar frame-and-panel construction with leather-lined panels.

Frame member

Amboyna burl over walnut veneer

This wedding chest by Miguel Gómez-Ibáñez for his son and daughter-in-law incorporates 43 panels of different sizes. Gómez-Ibáñez made them by gluing two layers of veneer over the outside face of each walnut core. On the inside face he applied one layer of veneer and, after the sides were assembled, a layer of burgundy leather.

out of it. He had managed to turn an intriguing idea into something that was "lifeless and boring."

"I was regularizing it," he writes, "that is to say, I was drawing many of the stiles and rails the same dimension and making many of the panels the same size." It was, he says, as if he was subconsciously making the chest easier to build than what the original sketch had suggested.

Those drawings went in the trash. He started again, first enlarging the napkin sketch and then drawing a grid over it so he could capture the same nuances in a set of full-scale construction drawings. When he was finished, he saw that nearly every rail and stile was of a different dimension and no two panels were exactly the same size.

With sides and front gently curved, construction was a stiff technical challenge that required Gómez-Ibáñez

to keep track of dozens of different pieces that varied only slightly. Hinges were designed by Gómez-Ibáñez and made by his son in titanium.

Gómez-Ibáñez is an architect turned furniture maker who attended the North Bennet Street School in Boston and now works with three other graduates in a collective shop in Waltham, Mass.

He says he is influenced by just about every furniture maker he's run into, especially those whose work is nothing like his own. When he's making furniture for himself, Gómez-Ibáñez says he finds ideas in 18th-century or earlier designs, but these days the furniture professional doesn't have much time for outside commissions. Since 2006, Gómez-Ibáñez has been executive director at his alma mater, North Bennet Street.

Size: 18 in. deep, 42 in. wide, 20 in. tall

Materials: Walnut, amboyna burl veneer, leather, titanium

Finish: Linseed oil, Waterlox, and wax

Contact: Gomez-ibanez@msn.org

Sheet Music Cabinet

Christopher Solar

A hobbyist furniture maker for a decade before turning professional only two years ago, Christopher Solar chose the design for this cabinet partly because it would give him a chance to make curved, veneered doors. "This client wanted a cabinet to store piano sheet music," Solar writes. "The overall dimensions were constrained by the intended location, but otherwise I more or less had free rein."

With their sweeping lines of inlay, the four doors became the centerpiece for the cabinet. Solar started by making a single-core panel with layers of 3mm Russian birch plywood, then added face veneers and solid-wood edging.

Solar even fabricated the brass pulls from brass bar stock. He roughed out the curves on a bandsaw, finished them up with a stationary belt sander, and formed the dimples with a router.

To arrive at the design for the cabinet, Solar went from rough sketches to a computer drawing and finally a full-scale drawing of the cabinet front on a piece of white melamine. "That let me prop it against a wall, stand back, and get a sense of the scale of the piece," he says. "I made the piece slightly bigger as a result."

Solar works in a basement shop at home in Ontario, Canada, a space he says is about as small as a furniture shop can get. His essential machinery includes a vacuum press and a dust collector.

Size: 16 in. deep, 53 in. wide, 29½ in. tall

Materials: Walnut, maple and curly maple veneers, wenge, medium-density fiberboard, brass

Finish: Interior: shellac and waterborne lacquer; exterior: Waterlox

Contact: www.christophersolar.com

10 Small Boxes Huddled Together for Warmth

Clark Kellogg

Houston, Texas, furniture maker Clark Kellogg is moving from grand scale to small scale. After graduating from the Center for Furniture Craftsmanship in Maine, Kellogg says he found himself veering toward smaller, friendlier pieces that revealed themselves in their details.

This wall cabinet was part of Kellogg's study there, an assignment to build a case piece in solid wood with at least one drawer and one door. He was inspired by a piece by J.P. Vilkman he had seen in a book, and he began drawing boxes—dozens and dozens of them.

"The more I drew, the more I started thinking about each box as a living thing," Kellogg says. "I had a great time thinking about all the little rules that would govern how the boxes should live together. Once the rules were in place, it felt like the cabinet practically drew itself."

He had one piece of cherry to work with, and it was barely enough. With no room for mistakes, Kel-

Clark Kellogg assembled 10 separate boxes into a single cabinet in a number of glue-ups, starting with pairs of adjacent boxes. He separated boxes with ⅛-in. ebonized spacers to create thin, uniform shadow lines.

logg was careful to orient the grain so that it wrapped around each box, and to come up with an "extremely detailed" cutting diagram.

And the name? Thought up in an instant as he looked out the window at a mid-February Maine landscape.

Size: 10½ in. deep, 18 in. wide, 24 in. tall

Materials: Cherry, maple

Finish: Waterlox tung-oil thinner mix

Contact: www.kelloggfurniture.com

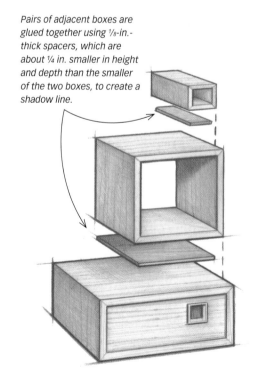

Pairs of adjacent boxes are glued together using ⅛-in.-thick spacers, which are about ¼ in. smaller in height and depth than the smaller of the two boxes, to create a shadow line.

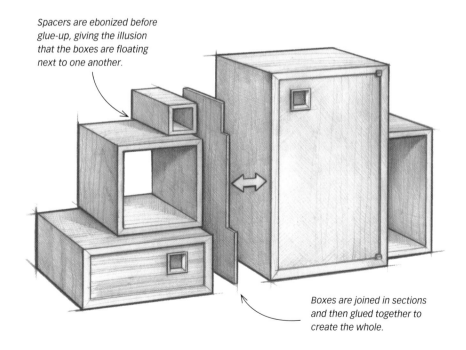

Spacers are ebonized before glue-up, giving the illusion that the boxes are floating next to one another.

Boxes are joined in sections and then glued together to create the whole.

Gingko Bookcase

Pat Morrow

A client of Colorado furniture maker Pat Morrow wanted to surprise his wife with a bookcase on their 25th anniversary. She loved gingko leaves as well as reading, and the client sent Morrow photos of both their living room and other bookcases he liked to get the design process rolling.

"My challenge was designing something that fit with his image but was my original idea," Morrow says. "I sent him several different sketches, we narrowed it down to three, and then I coaxed him into choosing this one."

Morrow says the client kept all of the emails the two traded during the design process, printed them out, and gave them to his wife. A brass plate inside the bookcase reads, "Grow old with me, the best is yet to come."

Morrow has been making furniture for six years and works in a two-car garage warmed by a pellet stove. "The one thing I do is work everything out on paper before I start cutting pieces," she says. "It helps me see where issues may be or change something for the better."

Size: 16½ in. deep, 42 in. wide, 66 in. tall

Materials: Cherry

Finish: Tung oil varnish

Contact: www.trailmixstudio.com

Jimmy's Buffet

Jim Postell

Jim Postell, a teacher of furniture design as well as a furniture maker, says his style and preferences have changed over the last two decades but he's settled into a comfortable familiarity with Baltic-birch plywood and solid cherry lumber.

Materials and fabrication techniques have had the largest impact on his style, he writes. "I tend to try to visually disassociate elements from one another, often through a recessed and dark reveal."

Such is the case with Jimmy's Buffet, which consists of five different-shaped storage components divided from one another visually with the help of black neoprene. Clear acrylic casters help separate the buffet visually from the floor. Postell says the interlocking free-form components are similar to Tetris®, a video game.

"The buffet enables a variety of uses," he says, "and celebrates the notion of part-to-whole relationships."

Postell has taught at the University of Cincinnati for the last 15 years and works in a two-story studio he says was inspired by a visit to George Nakashima's workshop many years ago.

Size: 21 in. deep, 66 in. wide, 36 in. tall

Materials: ⅛-in. bending plywood, cherry, neoprene, full-extension slides

Finish: Waterlox, waterborne poly-acrylic

Contact: jim.postell@uc.edu

Ark

Roger Savatteri

Roger Savatteri built this cabinet (also called an ark) for the Malibu Jewish Community Center and Synagogue in Malibu, Calif., not only to protect liturgical scrolls but also to serve as a spiritual focal point for the synagogue. The aim was to allow members of the congregation to see the scrolls while the doors were closed and to provide easy access to them during the service.

"I prepared designs for several possible combinations of wood and glass until I envisioned the wood itself could act as the medium through which light would penetrate," Savatteri writes. "This was the key that unlocked the design you see before you."

Using blueprint enlargements, Savatteri refined the stylized leaf pattern and then experimented with laser equipment to get the right depth of cut in sectional, full-scale laminations of the same materials the doors would be made from. The result makes it appear that the scrolls float within the cabinet.

Savatteri studied fine arts and industrial design, designed and built stage props, worked as a model maker and fabricator, and eventually opened a studio in Santa Monica. He now has a 1,500-sq.-ft. shop in Malibu.

Size: 39 in. deep, 78 in. wide, 94 in. tall

Materials: Acacia, koa, Spanish cedar, olive, poplar, birch plywood, acrylic, stainless steel, laminated bent-glass panels

Contact: www.savatteridesigns.com

Blanket Chest

Curtis Minier

Curtis Minier was pressed for time. As he was building his home on Vashon Island, Wash., the Northwest Fine Woodworking Gallery in Seattle scheduled its 25th-anniversary show, and Minier, one of its founding members, wanted to participate.

"So I decided to design and build a simple blanket chest," he says. "To add elegance to the piece, I incorporated a pattern that I designed using marquetry. This was both fun and challenging for me as I had never before done any marquetry."

Minier's design process typically would include presenting clients with as many rounds of design drawings as necessary. But in this instance, he simply built the chest from scale drawings.

Minier's favorite designer is Wendell Castle, who he admires for "always pushing the limits." He says his own style has evolved from the "California roundover style" he was taught three decades ago to something more contemporary. (Curtis Minier's chair is on pp. 62-63.)

Size: 20 in. deep, 58 in. wide, 22 in. tall

Materials: Curly maple and wenge veneer, wenge, bloodwood

Finish: Lacquer

Contact: curtminier@gmail.com

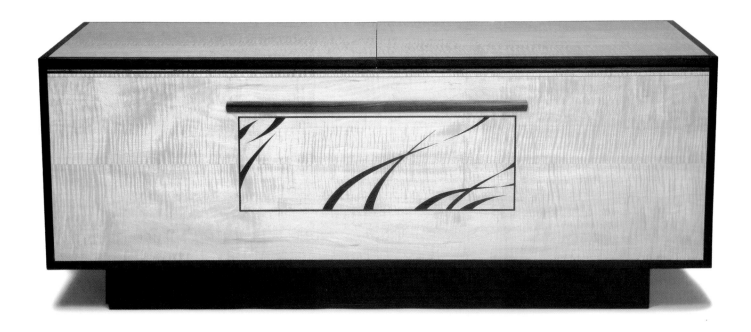

Tall Chest

Jason Schneider

It was a stack of pristine cardboard boxes that got Jason Schneider thinking. The boxes had been for new fluorescent light fixtures in the shop at Anderson Ranch Arts Center in Colorado, where Schneider is woodshop manager, and he just couldn't bring himself to throw them in the recycling bin.

So he started making furniture. This tall chest of drawers is constructed mostly of cardboard, cut to shape and stack-laminated in sections with yellow glue. In plan, the chest's curved face extends beyond the confines of the ash frame.

"It's really a great material to work with," Schneider says, with a few caveats. After it's been glued up, the front of the cabinet can be sanded but Schneider warns that it creates a lot of dust. It's also fragile during construction, making it a challenge to move around the shop without damage.

Finally, there's the question of cats. Cats? Scratching posts are sometimes made from cardboard, Schneider says, which would make him a little nervous selling such a piece to clients with cats in the house.

Working one section at a time, Jason Schneider glued sheets of corrugated cardboard together to create the carcase for this chest. Pieces are cut oversize when they are glued up and trimmed to final size before the sections are put together. Recesses for drawers are simply voids.

Size: 13 in. deep, 17 in. wide, 70 in. tall

Materials: Corrugated cardboard, ash, milk paint, gold leaf

Finish: Oil

Contact: www.jasonschneiderfurniture.com

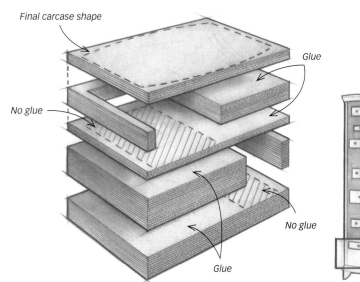

Final carcase shape

Glue

No glue

No glue

Glue

Keyboard Console

James Schriber

This wenge console by James Schriber looks like it could have been designed in the mid 20th century, even if the electronic keyboard and speakers it conceals are completely contemporary.

"A lot of what I make is coming out of the middle of the century," Schriber says, "not so much in a conscious way but in my subconscious."

One challenge with this piece, commissioned for a New York City client, was that it had to work as a decorative piece of furniture 90% of the time and only occasionally be transformed into a musical instrument. Blending these functional and aesthetic requirements took some doing.

As he did with most of his commissions, Schriber presented a handful of proposals to the prospective client. While some versions were more stylized, this understated version was the winner. He says his design process "is not pretty," but includes rough sketches, full-scale drawings, and building prototypes.

Schriber works with two employees in a 2,000-sq.-ft. commercial condo in New Milford, Conn. A professional furniture maker for 30 years, Schriber has demonstrated tremendous range in everything from beds and chairs to a special-edition pearwood Steinway called "Pianissimo." Asked to describe how his style and preferences have changed over the years, he has this one-word answer: "Cleaner."

Size: 22 in. deep, 88 in. wide, 33 in. tall

Materials: Wenge with cast bronze hardware

Finish: Oil and wax

Contact: www.jamesschriber.com

Ash Sideboard

Duncan Gowdy

Duncan Gowdy got the idea for this sideboard after a visit to coastal California. He and Wendy Maruyama had gone there to remember fellow furniture maker Michael Pierschalla. Gowdy returns to the spot when he's in the area. "On a visit late at night," he writes, "I could only see the white parts of the waves and the pattern of the receding water. The rest was black. The image stuck in my head and eventually became the carving on the front of the sideboard."

Gowdy, who works in a 625-sq.-ft. shop in Shelburne, Mass., was an illustration major in college before switching to furniture. At first, he carried over his earlier training and produced furniture that he described as, in essence, "three-dimensional illustrations."

Later, Gowdy developed an appreciation for Shaker furniture and a more minimalist approach, which he combines with relief carving and painted images.

Rushing to complete this sideboard, Gowdy bungled the finish on the doors. Rather than trying to fix them, he says he made the doors over again.

Size: 18 in. deep, 53 in. wide, 33 in. tall

Materials: Ash, quartersawn white oak

Finish: Pickling stain, gel polyurethane stain, oil

Contact: www.duncangowdy.com

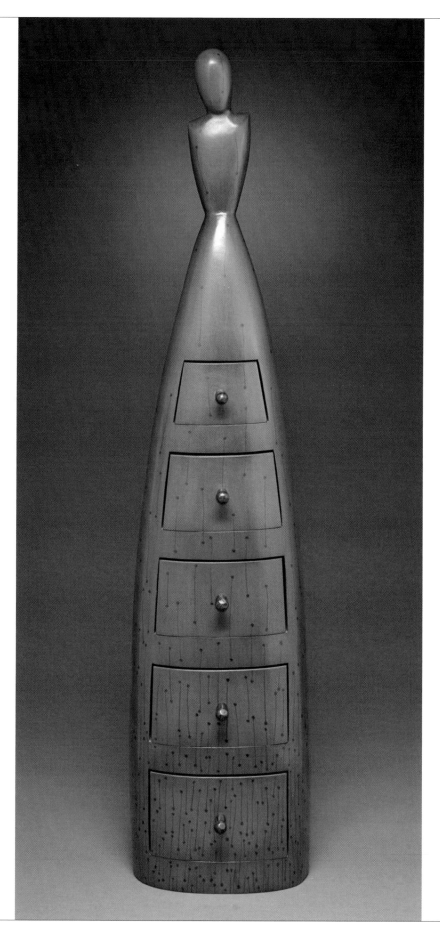

Shed
Kimberly Winkle

Kimberly Winkle was invited to take part in an exhibition in Santa Fe, N.M., called "Weather or Not" and chose to submit something inspired by autumn. She describes this diminutive chest as suggestive of both a human, who might be shedding secrets or feelings, and a tree that would be shedding leaves at that time of year.

A master's graduate from San Diego State University, Winkle has been a furniture maker for nine years and says her style has become more relaxed over time. "My graduate work was stiff and austere with a serious tone," she writes. "My work is now is lighthearted with a strong emphasis on color, form, and line."

She and her husband, also a woodworker, share a 1,200-sq.-ft. shop behind their home in Smithville, Tenn. It has a shared machine room and bathroom but separate studios.

"I like to listen to loud and rowdy music in my studio while I'm working, but my husband likes to listen to quiet and calm classical music while he's working," she says. "So he bought me an iPod® to solve this problem. Rock on!"

Size: 6 in. deep, 9 in. wide, 34 in. tall

Materials: Poplar

Finish: Milk paint, graphite, spray polyurethane

Contact: wimkinkle@yahoo.com

Audio Cabinet

Jon Francis

A schoolteacher by profession, Jon Francis has been a part-time furniture maker for 20 years, long enough to see his tastes run from Chippendale and Queen Anne through Mission and Arts and Crafts, and finally to a more contemporary style with an Asian flavor.

When it came time to make something for his own audio equipment, Francis says he "wanted a cabinet with a clean, unadorned design built with strong horizontal lines." He chose sliding doors over hinged doors to keep the look contemporary, and divided each door into three panels to add some vertical lines to the cabinet face.

Francis says he typically works from scale drawings rather than full-scale drawings or mock-ups. "I alter design as I build," he says, "and especially focus on proportion of all elements by seeing the piece from different angles." Francis works in a 20-ft. by 35-ft. shop next to his Fayetteville, Ark., home. Teaching keeps him busy enough during the year to keep big projects waiting until his summer break.

Size: 17 in. deep, 50 in. wide, 29 in. tall

Materials: Local black cherry, dyed white oak, burlap

Finish: Oil-varnish mix

Contact: francisjoinery@cox.net

Open Hutch

Peter Turner

This hutch is really part of a matched pair that Peter Turner built for clients who did not have enough floor space in their dining room to accommodate one large cabinet.

Well, nearly matched. The mate to this one, on the same long wall of the room and separated by a window, does not have the open space beneath the upper cabinet. Turner included the opening in this cabinet to provide a little extra counter space.

The design had its start 10 years ago when Turner built a commissioned hutch and incorporated a few elements he's seen in linen presses from the Shaker community at Pleasant Hill, Ky. He has been refining it ever since.

Turner made the wide cove at the top of the cabinet on the tablesaw by running 6/4 stock over the blade at an angle, raising the blade incrementally until he had the curve he wanted. The molding is attached to a frame that can be removed from the hutch when it's being transported.

The hutch was built from scale drawings. Ordinarily, Turner says, he would move to full-size drawings before construction, but he was familiar enough with the piece to skip that step this time. (For a look at Turner's armchair, see pp. 90-91.)

Size: 15 in. deep, 34 in. wide, 76 in. tall

Material: Cherry, soft maple

Finish: Mix of spar varnish, tung oil, and citrus thinner

Contact: www.petersturner.com

Vanity

Leah Woods

Before starting work on this project, Leah Woods had finished a series of cabinets in which the lines and shapes of women's clothing were translated into doors, legs, and cabinet pulls. "I began to explore the bigger issue of thinking about one's own beauty," she says, "and how women (as well as men) make choices about how they want to present themselves to the world."

The result was Vanity, a desk and chair combination that Woods says is designed to create an intimate atmosphere for making decisions about appearance.

"I really wanted this piece to communicate a sense of privacy, where someone could let her most vulnerable feelings show," she says.

Woods, a teacher at the University of New Hampshire, works in the university's shop and rents studio space in the Button Factory, a former mill in Portsmouth, N.H., that's now home to a number of artisans.

Size: Desk: 29 in. deep, 44 in. wide, 46 in. tall; Chair: 26 in. deep, 22 in. wide, 33 in. tall

Materials: Walnut, Australian walnut veneer, Africa satinwood veneer, brass hardware

Finish: Black dye and gel varnish

Contact: www.leahwoodsstudio.com

CASE GOODS

Size: 17¼ in. deep, 64 in. wide, 38 in. tall

Materials: Burl laurel and curly ash veneer over MDF, poplar, and honeycomb cores, shedua, ebony, walnut

Finish: Shellac, polyurethane varnish

Contact: www.slnatof.com

Reveal here suggests area to the left is part of side.

Cardboard honeycomb reduces weight.

³/₁₆-in. MDF skin, glued over poplar or cardboard honeycomb

Poplar blocking, ¾ in. thick (end grain showing)

By using veneer instead of solid lumber, Lloyd Natof can manipulate how his furniture is perceived. Wrapping veneer around a mitered corner and onto the top, for example, makes the sides appear massively thick. The substrate for veneer is a mix of poplar and cardboard honeycomb, surfaced with ³/₁₆-in. MDF.

Amarelo Buffet
S. Lloyd Natof

Chicago furniture maker S. Lloyd Natof likes to work with spectacular veneer and challenge himself to make something as simple as a box be more than just a box.

"It is important that the veneer pattern is not just surface decoration," he says. "It has to somehow lock into the piece and transform our sense of the case. The brick pattern presented itself as a static textural effect that would look interesting held between the book-matched sides."

Natof says he got interested in wrapping veneer around a mitered edge about 10 years ago when he realized the technique allowed him to "work with volumes" rather than planks. He admits, however, that folding a box together after the panels have been mitered and veneered can mean an anxious day or two.

Natof used cardboard honeycomb as well as medium-density fiberboard and poplar for the core of the box to keep it lighter (see drawing). He works from rough sketches and doesn't build prototypes. "I need to see and handle the actual materials," he says.

I See Fish, I See Ties

Michael Cullen

This toy chest began with a carved wall hanging, which Michael Cullen had time to reconsider while lying in bed suffering from a nasty bout of the flu. When he was back on his feet, Cullen improved on the panel. The more vibrant colors that resulted enhanced the playful nature of the design and, before long, Cullen was planning a toy chest to go with it.

Cullen, a professional who has been making furniture for 22 years, draws on the work of many artisans, including David Powell, John Makepeace, Judy McKie, Richard Riemerschmid, and James Krenov. Rather than adopting a single, unvarying style, Cullen says his preferences change constantly and may encompass everything from the natural-wood furniture of George Nakashima to the more flamboyant work of Carlo Bugatti, a versatile Italian artist and furniture maker who died in 1940.

Trained by David Powell at the Leeds Design Workshops in Easthampton, Mass., and later at Emily Street Workshops in Cambridge, Mass., Cullen now works in a 2,400-sq.-ft. shop in Petaluma, Calif. He likes industrial-scale woodworking equipment supplemented by traditional hand tools. Cullen usually works by himself on his pieces, although he does take one or two full-time apprentices each year.

Cullen often works with both full-scale drawings and mock-ups, although in this case a "loose" full-scale drawing was enough to keep him on track through construction without dimming the spontaneity of the design. A sample carved leg helped him fine-tune the design, but otherwise Cullen built no prototype.

In addition to the carved top, important design details are borrowed from Arts and Crafts furniture, including solid-wood construction and exposed joinery. For Cullen, the single most challenging part of the design was integrating the body of the chest with the top.

Size: 18 in. deep, 32 in. wide, 24 in. tall

Materials: Carved solid mahogany, purpleheart battens, Port Orford cedar bottom

Finish: Milk paint with shellac overcoat; interior, clear shellac

Contact: www.michaelcullendesign.com

Lingerie Chest

Steve Holman

Vermont furniture maker Steve Holman was approached at the Philadelphia Furniture Show by a couple who wanted to commission a chest similar to one he had made on spec a few years before (and later sold at a deep discount at a gallery).

The result was this lingerie chest whose top drawer is high enough to require a matching stool. The case is spline-mitered following the technique taught by Tage Frid. The triangular recesses were routed using a template.

Holman has been a professional furniture maker for 27 years and now finds himself more interested in the end result than the process. "I went through a period when I thought I could be a great *artiste* and produced a lot of spec work that reflected my own artistic vision," he writes. "Alas, the furniture world seemed not to share my creative ideals, and most of that great visionary work is now in my house or sold through galleries at tremendous discount."

These days Holman takes a more practical point of view, counting himself lucky to do "good and interesting" work in whatever style his clients want.

Size: 26 in. deep, 26 in. wide, 77 in. tall (stool is 16 in. square, 12 in. tall)

Materials: Figured soft maple, purpleheart, nogal, mahogany

Finish: Precatalyzed lacquer

Contact: www.holmanstudios.com

Credenza

Craig Jentz

This credenza, designed to house stereo equipment, is a replacement for an angular Danish modern predecessor, a reflection of Craig Jentz's growing appreciation for curved lines and the potential of bent laminations.

Jentz combined cherry and tiger maple so the credenza would match a pair of tiger-maple sofas and a cherry dining set he had made years earlier that were displayed in an adjacent room.

An amateur furniture maker for more than 20 years, Jentz says he works from a combination of rough drawings and models. "For me, it is very difficult to visualize curved surfaces on paper," he writes. "I need the models to see the true perspective and determine what does and doesn't look right. Most of the details are worked out ad hoc as I go."

Jentz works in a 475-sq.-ft. basement shop. After living in Europe for several years, he decided inches and fractions didn't make much sense for furniture making. He's since converted to the metric system.

Size: 24 in. deep, 80 in. wide, 30 in. tall

Materials: Cherry, tiger maple

Finish: Lacquer

Sir Gilbert's Chest

Don Green

D on Green has a number of things in mind as he designs furniture, not only a visual composition that stylistically will remain current and appealing (what Green calls "timeless" design) but also something that will be marketable and affordable.

This tall chest, with its alternating blocks of sapele and its simple, ebonized base, was designed as part of a collection that Green could make in multiples. (See Miss Olivia's Writing Desk on pp. 96-97 and Lady Edith's Bench on pp. 74-75.)

Many of Green's pieces are named for family members or close friends. But Sir Gilbert? No close relation, as it turns out. Green's wife and business partner, Jenifer, says Sir Gilbert is just "a handsome name that suited the piece."

Size: 21 in. deep, 34 in. wide, 72 in. tall

Materials: Ebonized mahogany, maple, sapele, rubber-and-metal drawer pulls

Finish: Nitrocellulose lacquer

Contact: www.greentreehome.com

Cantilevered Cabinet

Todd Ouwehand

Los Angeles furniture maker Todd Ouwehand's original goal was to build a cabinet that seemed to defy gravity. "My first thought was to have a single angled support that was obviously incapable of keeping the cabinet upright and give the piece stability by bolting it to the wall," he writes. "I realized that it would be a greater accomplishment if I could get that result and have the cabinet freestanding."

What grew out of this notion was a cantilevered cabinet with asymmetrical doors (inside, there are two drawers and three shelves). The stiffest challenge was getting the right spacing between vertical dividers on the doors; the pattern on the smaller door is a compressed version of the other.

Ouwehand says he always works from full-scale drawings and, for him, the design process also includes "several sketches, scale drawings, and plenty of contemplation." Although he sometimes builds prototypes, he did not in this case.

Ouwehand, who studied at California State University Long Beach, says he especially admires the work of John Nyquist and George Nakashima. He has been a furniture maker since 1983.

Size: 16 in. deep, 43 in. wide, 52 in. tall

Materials: Walnut, zebrawood veneer

Finish: Oil

Contact: www.toddouwehand.com

Claro Walnut Sideboard

Ted Blachly

Ted Blachly's clients knew exactly how big their new sideboard would have to be, but as to the rest of the design they were open to suggestions. Maybe best of all, they did not insist on a rigid timetable for its completion.

"Smart move," Blachly says. "I work very slowly and carefully at the beginning of a project, the design stages primarily. I'm not satisfied too easily and find that if I allow myself the time to explore and try to see what will be good for the whole piece, it's worth the time."

Blachly first completed a series of sketches to serve as a starting point for further discussions. Ordinarily, wood choices would spring from the clients' desire for a particular color, but in this case they had seen other Blachly pieces in claro walnut and asked specifically about it. Claro comes from the stumps of orchard walnuts, its rich, multi-toned figure a result of grafting the upper part of the tree to a different rootstock.

"Working with big slabs of claro walnut is very humbling," he writes. "The wood comes from very old trees, which may have defects, but the grain patterns are quite varied so cutting parts is an important step. There is a chance to compose."

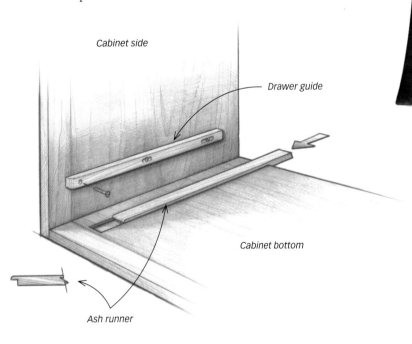

Cabinet side

Drawer guide

Cabinet bottom

Ash runner

Instead of a traditional web frame in the bottom of his sideboard, Ted Blachly cut two 3/16-in.-deep, tapered dovetail sockets for ash runners. The runners, 1/8 in. proud of the surface, are wide enough for the drawer to glide on.

Sketches, full-scale drawings, and mock-ups all play a role in Blachly's design process, but not always in that order. Although he prefers to start construction with a set of full-scale drawings, Blachly may find he needs to mock up a particular part in midstream to test design or construction ideas. Then it's back to the drawing board. When the drawings are complete, he makes a quick prototype from framing lumber.

Blachly, a professional furniture maker with a 1,300-sq.-ft. basement shop in Warner, N.H., took a single furniture course in college and worked in old-house carpentry for a decade before rediscovering an interest in cabinet-making and furniture. He credits both Sam Maloof and John McAlevey with design inspiration but says his most influential teacher has been Jere Osgood, a fellow member of the New Hampshire Furniture Masters Association for whom he once worked as an assistant.

Size: 19 in. deep, 66 in. wide, 33 in. tall

Materials: Claro walnut, ebonized cherry, curly maple, rosewood

Finish: Exterior, varnish; interior, shellac

Contact: www.tedblachly.com

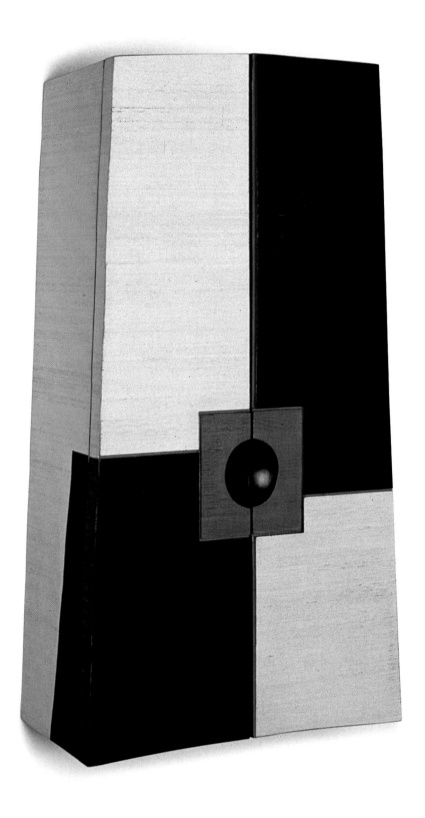

Wall Cabinet

Susan Working

S usan Working calls this wall cabinet an experiment, and that description is in keeping with an approach to furniture making that leaves room for the unexpected.

"I'm very interested in the process of making," she writes. "I'm not very interested in planning detailed preliminary drawings or in controlling outcomes. I don't know exactly where I'm going when I start. By setting up a kind of 'conversation' with the materials, I can allow unexpected things to come in from the side."

Working, the director of the Furniture Design and Woodworking program at Anderson Ranch Arts Center in Colorado, says that was not always the case. For years, she worked more conventionally, and with more traditional designs.

"In recent years," she adds, "I've become more interested in the expressive potential of furniture, particularly in the way it can be used as a metaphor for the body."

Size: 5½ in. deep, 12½ in. wide, 24½ in. tall

Materials: Cherry, glass

Finish: Paint, gold leaf, shellac

Contact: www.susanworking.com

Temple Cabinet

Timothy Coleman

Timothy Coleman knew the carved door panels would be a focal point of this cabinet. "I am fascinated with Chinese lattice designs and this pattern draws a lot of inspiration from that realm," Coleman says. "I pay a lot of attention to the simple lines of Chinese furniture and I try to echo this in my own work."

Temple Cabinet also combines two woods that contrast subtly with each other, cherry and yew. Coleman says that while they are similar in tone, the two have different grain patterns. He was especially drawn to yew for its "perfect combination of tone and texture" for this piece, but he had only a limited amount to work with. To stretch the yew far enough, Coleman cut it into veneer and laid up the panels.

"There is a raw, woody feeling to yew wood," Coleman says, "but at the same time it takes on a beautiful luster when finished."

(For a look at more of Coleman's work, see his settee on p. 65 and a pair of side tables on p. 17.)

Size: 15 in. deep, 32 in. wide, 51 in. tall

Materials: Cherry legs, frames, top; yew panels, cedar interior drawers

Finish: Shellac

Contact: www.timothycoleman.com

Size: 9 in. deep, 15 in. wide, 32 in. tall

Materials: Quartersawn white oak, veneer, brass

Finish: Polyacrylic

Contact: blaisdelldesign@gmail.com

DVD Cabinet

Nate Blaisdell

This DVD cabinet by Nate Blaisdell was designed to fulfill a practical need without detracting from its surroundings. "While working with the scale, proportions, and my overall visual idea," Blaisdell writes, "I had to maintain the structural integrity of the cabinet. The three-way mitered base proved difficult when balancing those issues."

Cabinet shelves are profiled to match the outside of the doors so the two can nestle when the doors are closed. This detail was part of Blaisdell's effort to create a direct relationship between the inside and outside of the cabinet.

Blaisdell has been making furniture for five years and has recently turned professional. The simple elegance of Danish furniture has been a major design influence, although he adds that the work and commitment of Wharton Esherick have had the most impact on him.

Currently shopless, the Annapolis, Md., furniture maker says he hopes to be building one soon. (A chair by Nate Blaisdell appears on p. 89.)

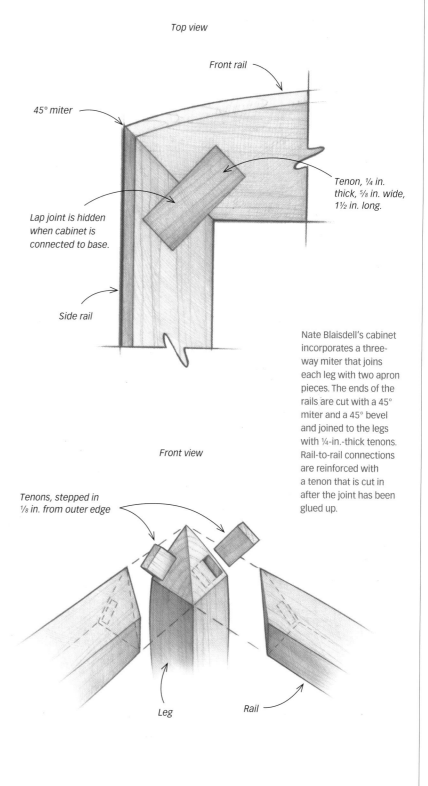

Top view

Front rail

45° miter

Tenon, ¼ in. thick, ⅝ in. wide, 1½ in. long.

Lap joint is hidden when cabinet is connected to base.

Side rail

Nate Blaisdell's cabinet incorporates a three-way miter that joins each leg with two apron pieces. The ends of the rails are cut with a 45° miter and a 45° bevel and joined to the legs with ¼-in.-thick tenons. Rail-to-rail connections are reinforced with a tenon that is cut in after the joint has been glued up.

Front view

Tenons, stepped in ⅛ in. from outer edge

Leg

Rail

Entry Sideboard

Seth Barrett

The idea for this sideboard grew out of an assignment Seth Barrett had been given in school and confirmed his faith in preserving design ideas in a sketchbook. "It is a great way to generate new ideas and work through issues in ongoing work," he says. "Almost no one can say they don't have 10 minutes a day to open a sketchbook."

Barrett says he was working with the idea of inserting functional components inside open structures. In developing this design with the client, bluestone became the material of choice for the top. The stone, Barrett says, helps bridge the gap between interior and exterior environments.

One change he'd consider in making the sideboard again is choosing a material for the door panels and drawer fronts more closely related to the ash cases. "This might increase the visual difference between structural elements and functional areas," he says.

Size: 15 in. deep, 48 in. wide, 36 in. tall

Materials: Walnut, ash, zebrawood, ash veneer, bluestone

Finish: Oil, lacquer

Contact: sethbarrett@earthlink.net

Lines Lowboard

Jari-Pekka Vilkman

Jari-Pekka Vilkman sees his Lines lowboard as a starting point for future work, its clean lines opening the door to many decorative possibilities.

"I can use it like a canvas that I paint again," he says. "The form is right and I just need to change the appearance. A flower marquetry version is already designed, and I would like to make a version where I can play with colors."

As he does with all of his work, Vilkman started with a few rough sketches and then built a mock-up, which he says is the only way to make sure the proportions will be right. The case is made from veneer over medium-density fiberboard.

Size: 18 in. deep, 80 in. wide, 18 in. tall

Materials: Walnut, birch, ash, bog oak, medium-density fiberboard

Finish: Lacquer

Contact: www.j-pvilkman.com

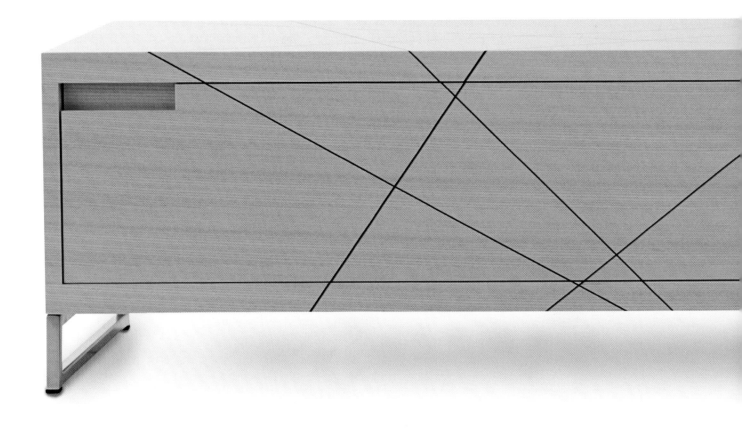

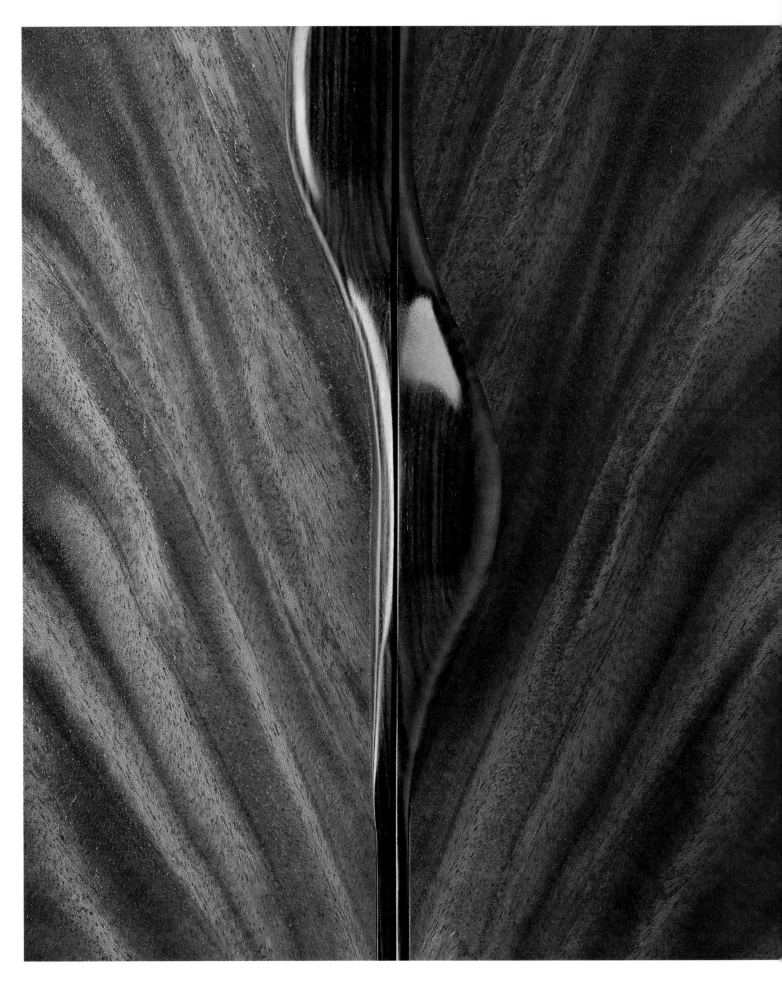

ACCESSORIES

Most pieces of furniture are functional in an obvious way—chairs for sitting, desks for working, beds for sleeping. We use these things every day, but other objects play more of a supporting role.

We were struck by the complexity of design and execution in the accessories we have included here. The boxes are actually small case pieces whose joinery becomes all the more difficult when dovetails, dadoes, and mortises and tenons are measured in fractions of an inch. Design, too, can be a challenge, not only in engineering small objects so they function properly but also in giving them proportions that make them look natural even if they are small.

Accessories don't always require much in the way of raw materials, and they may, in truth, be things we could live without. But they can hold special delight and help make a room seem complete.

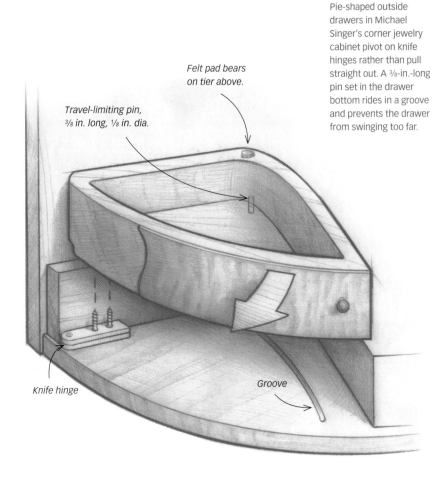

Travel-limiting pin,
3/8 in. long, 1/8 in. dia.

Felt pad bears
on tier above.

Pie-shaped outside drawers in Michael Singer's corner jewelry cabinet pivot on knife hinges rather than pull straight out. A 3/8-in.-long pin set in the drawer bottom rides in a groove and prevents the drawer from swinging too far.

Knife hinge

Groove

Jewelry Cabinet

Michael Singer

The skin of crotch-grain mahogany on the doors of this corner jewelry cabinet would be a commanding presence anywhere, part of Michael Singer's aim to build a cabinet that was "visually bold" without taking up much floor space in a small dressing area.

Singer, a self-taught professional in California, sketched out a few ideas on paper before turning to computer software to refine his design and work out details to scale. Doors are form-bent laminations veneered on the inside with plain-cut mahogany. Inside, the 15 small drawers are milled from solid blocks of hard maple.

Singer says that because the cabinet is wedge-shaped, the outer drawers in each bank pivot rather than pull out. Drawers ride on a knife hinge with their swing controlled by a pin in an arc-shaped groove (see drawing). Working out the mechanics of the drawer was the toughest part of the project.

Singer works out of a 600-sq.-ft. garage at home with only a single piece of stationary equipment—his tablesaw. Everything else is on wheels. Singer says he started with "easy" Mission-style pieces, but adds, "I have found that as my technical skills and confidence have grown, it has allowed my designs to get more sophisticated. I use a lot more curves now."

Size: 20 in. deep, 20 in. wide, 63 in. tall

Materials: Mahogany, hard maple, ebony, silver cloth

Finish: Shellac and wax

Contact: www.msfinewoodworking.com

Variations on a Box

Greg Smith

Greg Smith had been wondering how he might incorporate round drawers in a rectilinear cabinet. As an exercise, he built some tube-shaped drawers, which kicked around his shop for a few years before he took the idea in a different direction. "At some point," he says, "it occurred to me that the thing to do would be to build a tube-shaped box with 'regular' drawers."

The result is his latest effort to explore the many variations of what a box can look like. Only 15½ in. wide, this one is constructed with traditional joinery. "The tricky part, of course, is doing this joinery in a round object," Smith says.

Smith has been a professional furniture maker for 20 years. He attended the College of the Redwoods in Fort Bragg, Calif., in the early 1990s and teaches there now.

In addition to being influenced by longtime College of the Redwoods teacher and furniture maker James Krenov, Smith says he has been inspired by furniture and other objects from the Ming dynasty of China.

Size: 8½ in. deep, 15½ in. wide, 8 in. tall

Materials: Afzelia, Deodar cedar, brass

Finish: Shellac, wax

Contact: www.gregbsmith.com

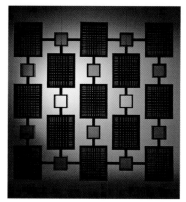

Quadrangles

Jennifer Anderson

Jennifer Anderson's goal with this hanging room divider was to create a sculptural object whose niches also could be used to display small objects. She combined panels made from woven strips of walnut veneer and a series of shallow boxes backed with stainless-steel screen, assembling the screen with threaded inserts and bolts.

Anderson worked quickly, moving directly from rough sketches to construction without scaled drawings or a prototype. She did, however, make several samples of the woven pattern to narrow down the number of options.

Anderson shares a cooperative shop in San Diego, Calif., with 10 other woodworkers. She studied environmental design in college, then furniture making at the College of the Redwoods with James Krenov, at San Diego State University with Wendy Maruyama, and in Sweden at the craft school founded by Carl Malmsten.

Along the way, Anderson has picked up an appreciation for the subtleties of hand-worked surfaces. "Before, the perfect consistency of the mass-produced look was my goal," she says. "Now, the subtle inconsistencies of the handmade are optimal." (For Anderson's chairs, see pp. 82-83).

Should she tackle a similar project in the future, Anderson says she would consider making the screen a floor piece instead of suspending it from the ceiling. This would make installation easier.

Size: 4½ in. deep, 72 in. wide, 72 in. tall

Materials: Wenge, walnut veneer, stainless-steel screen

Finish: Shellac

Contact: www.jenniferandersonstudio.com

Isabella's Treasures

Scott King

Most people looking at a photograph of this chest think of something much larger than it actually is, writes maker Scott King. In fact, the scale of the project is very small: The largest drawer is just over 2 in. tall and the diminutive cabinet measures only 15 in. wide.

King made the chest as a place for his 3-year-old daughter, Isabella, to keep the small but special objects she is likely to collect over the years. At the suggestion of his woodworking instructor, King took a look at a book on Japanese tansu furniture and found a starting point. "Though I was not particularly drawn to the hardware and general visual character of the tansu style," he says, "I quite liked the asymmetric layout of doors and drawers."

He used an extensive mock-up process to get dimensions and proportions right. With something so small, King found that moving something even $\frac{1}{32}$ in. made a real difference in how the chest looked.

In the end, he had to make a few chisels that were small enough to work on the dovetails for the drawers. Even the smallest commercially available hinges proved too big for the doors, so he made those, too. (A side chair by King appears on p. 76.)

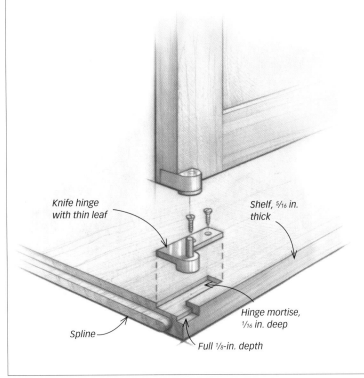

Knife hinge with thin leaf

Shelf, ⁵⁄₁₆ in. thick

Hinge mortise, ¹⁄₁₆ in. deep

Spline

Full ⅛-in. depth

The very small scale of Scott King's treasure box encouraged innovative thinking. King had to make his own hinges because commercially available hinges were too big. Nor was there room for a full-depth hinge mortise in a shelf only ⁵⁄₁₆ in. thick. So King modified this one so the leaf is at its full thickness only at the outside of the case.

Size: 6 in. deep, 15 in. wide, 8 in. tall

Materials: Beech, Spanish cedar, Douglas fir, red cabreuva, brass, steel

Finish: Shellac

Contact: www.scottkingfurniture.com

Three Sisters

David Upfill-Brown

There's nothing simple about this small veneered box by David Upfill-Brown. On one level, it was an exercise in designing a box that could be accessed from all sides, and to use a swinging-drawer devised by English master John Makepeace. But it also has a geographic theme, named for a group of mesas in South Africa. Finally, it represented a chance for Upfill-Brown to practice vacuum-bag veneering.

Upfill-Brown, a displaced Australian now teaching at the Center for Furniture Craftsmanship in Maine, found the box presented more than its fair share of technical challenges. Bending multiple layers of veneer and thin strips of hard maple through tight curves took some ingenuity.

Upfill-Brown has been making furniture for 36 years. He cites a long list of favorite craftsmen and artists, ranging from James Krenov to Judy Kensley McKie, as well as Art Deco, Art Nouveau, and Biedermeier designers, and even Zimbabwean stone sculptors.

"I came to furniture through sculpture," Upfill-Brown writes. "A career fulfilling the (mostly conservative) requirements of furniture clients is evolving steadily to allow me to reinvestigate and integrate with furniture these nascent sculptural interests." (A dining table by Upfill-Brown appears on pp. 30-31.)

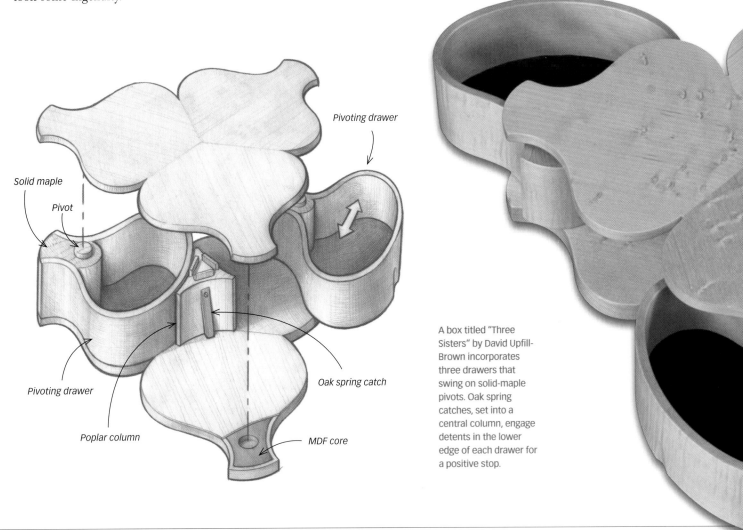

Solid maple

Pivot

Pivoting drawer

Pivoting drawer

Poplar column

MDF core

Oak spring catch

A box titled "Three Sisters" by David Upfill-Brown incorporates three drawers that swing on solid-maple pivots. Oak spring catches, set into a central column, engage detents in the lower edge of each drawer for a positive stop.

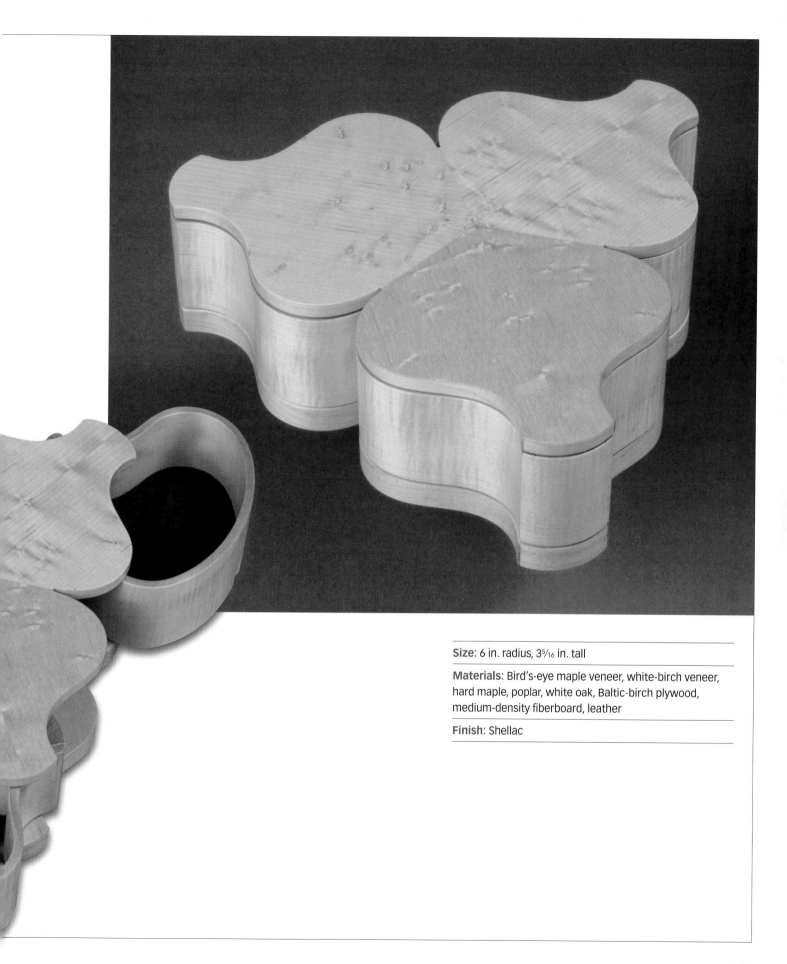

Size: 6 in. radius, 3⁵⁄₁₆ in. tall

Materials: Bird's-eye maple veneer, white-birch veneer, hard maple, poplar, white oak, Baltic-birch plywood, medium-density fiberboard, leather

Finish: Shellac

PRODUCTION
FURNITURE

Just because it's *not* one of a kind
doesn't make it boring

BY SCOTT GIBSON

Buttercup Rocker
22½ in. deep, 30¼ in. wide, 28 in. tall
Oak, brushed stainless steel
Blu Dot℠ Design & Manufacturing
www.bludot.com

Studio furniture makers usually design and build things one at a time, gathering materials for a single table or chest and seeing the process all the way through. It's a method of work that separates them from shops and factories capable of turning out dozens or hundreds of copies of the same thing in no time flat.

This single-handed process of turning raw materials into a finished piece of furniture elevates the maker over the mechanics of production; customers who buy the work are investing in the craftsman, not just the work. The expectation of getting something unique is what keeps many small furniture shops in business.

Tansu 7 Drawer Dresser
22 in. deep, 62 in. wide, 32 in. tall
Mahogany, figured cherry
Berkeley Mills℠
www.berkeleymills.com

Table Bench
21 in. deep, 55 in. wide, 30 in. tall (seat 16 in. tall)
Claro walnut, white oak, beeswax
Pieter VanTuyl
www.pietervantuyl.com

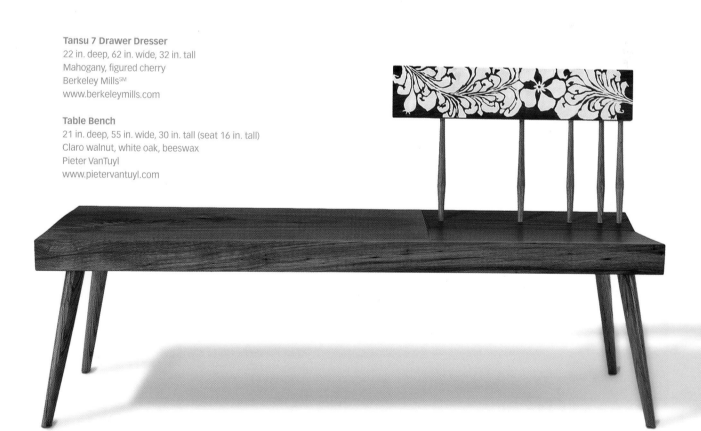

Curved Bed
Queen size: 65 in. wide, 87 in. long, 42 in. tall
FSC-certified cherry and tiger maple veneer
Woodshanti Cooperative Inc.
www.woodshanti.com

Stoller Dining Table
39 in. wide, 108 in. long, 29 in. tall
Walnut, steel, aluminum, stainless steel
www.stollerworks.com

At the other end of the spectrum are shops that specialize in turning out multiple copies of the same piece. They might be very large operations, places where lumber arrives and finished goods leave by tractor-trailer, or much smaller in scale. Although they might allow some customization, these shops are basically working from a set menu. For the sake of convenience, let's call these makers of multiples "production shops."

When someone buys this kind of furniture, there may be no way of telling who actually made it, and in some cases no way of knowing who designed it. And for that reason it would be easy to dismiss production furniture as bland or uninteresting, designed to offend the fewest number of potential buyers but lacking the originality and careful attention to detail found in the truly custom shop.

In reality, some production shops turn out an amazing variety of inventive, beautifully executed pieces of furniture using materials and techniques that are well beyond the scope of many small custom shops. If department stores and discount chains seem stuck on early American or gaudy French provincial, there also are many companies, even large ones, that use first-quality materials, innovative designs, and tightly controlled production methods.

JUST WHAT IS A 'PRODUCTION' SHOP?

It might be useful to start by looking a little more closely at what we mean by "production furniture." It's murkier than it seems. The term implies something made in an industrial setting where many people have a small part

Vita Dining Table
48 in. wide, 98 in. to 118 in. long, 30 in. tall
Solid cherry and cherry veneer, sycamore
Thos. Moser Cabinetmakers®
www.thosmoser.com

in the creation of a single piece of furniture. Speed matters, certainly, because time really is money. Economies of scale—that is, producing many identical parts for a given piece at the same time or buying raw materials in volume—are important because they, too, help keep costs down. Predictability and repeatability are key—they're basic tenets of modern manufacturing. Limiting opportunities for customers to alter basic designs makes the work go faster and thus be less expensive.

On the other hand, the single craftsman might take the time to match each and every board for figure and color, completely modify a standard design for a specific customer, or even deliver the piece personally.

But it's not as simple as dividing the furniture world into "custom" and "production." Even small shops may sometimes become production operations on occasion. For example, what about the one-artisan shop asked to make a dining set—a table, two armchairs, and six side chairs? Those six identical chairs (a matched set, after all) require 24 identical legs as well as multiples of many other parts. If the craftsman wants to make a profit, then speed, economies of scale, and repeatability all start to sound like good ideas.

PP68
Designed by Hans Wegner
18½ in. deep, 22¾ in. wide, 27½ in. tall (seat 17½ in. tall)
Ash, rush
Manufactured by PP Møbler, Denmark
Distributed in the U.S. by dkVogue, www.dkvogue.com

What about smaller shops that employ apprentices or journeymen to build the furniture designed by the owner? There are lots of shops like these, producing well-designed furniture that's not exactly cheap. The likes of Sam Maloof, Michael Fortune, Mira Nakashima, Ejler Hjorth-Westh, and Doug Green won't strike many of us as factory owners. If I buy a chair designed by George Nakashima and made now by a journeyman in the shop of Mira Nakashima, his daughter, does that make it a "factory piece?"

Moreover, big producers can make furniture that's as well known, and as pricey, as anything made in a custom shop. At the turn of the 20th century, the Craftsman Workshops of Gustav Stickley produced Mission furniture by the boatload. When you come across a genuine Stickley table or chair in an antique shop or auction house today, it won't be any bargain.

So in regard to the product that eventually emerges from a shop, the dividing line between small custom and production is fuzzy, not really a line at all but a gray zone.

Geo Low Tables
Designed by Arik Levy
16 in. to 34 in. wide, 21 in. to 36 in. long, 10 in. tall
Aluminum, wood veneer
Council Design
www.councildesign.com

Flute Bench
20 in. deep, 59 in. wide, 16 in. tall
White oak, leather
Julien Armand
www.julienarmand.com

DOES THE DEBATE EVER REALLY CHANGE?

And yet the debate over the merits of mass-produced vs. handmade, custom furniture has never really quieted down. Wallace Nutting, the critic, collector of American furniture, and author of the encyclopedic two-volume *Furniture Treasury*, called furniture "the most intimate of our permanent creations." He raged about the low-quality junk on the market and lamented the paucity of talented American cabinetmakers when the real talent came from Europe. If he didn't criticize the factory experience directly, he was adamant in believing it produced little of permanent value, in part because the buying public wouldn't know quality when staring it in the face.

"There is not anywhere a sufficient demand for really good furniture to warrant manufacturers in producing it," he wrote. "That is a cold, incontrovertible fact which has been proved by many serious, honorable, persistent attempts to produce such furniture. It is humiliating but none the less true that no amount of money can purchase in the shops furniture made in the best manner and applicable to all modern needs."

That was back in 1933, and even the cranky and unyielding Nutting would probably have no trouble finding people with the same point of view today.

There is something joyous and humanizing in the irregularities of handmade work, something charming in the idea that it was made by a person with a name and a face. The single artisan working alone still counts for something. But in the great tumble of mass-produced furniture in the marketplace today, finding something lively, interesting, and well made isn't a stretch, either. Just have a look at this collection, representing the output of production shops large and small. □

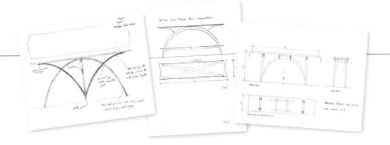

AN EXERCISE IN DESIGN

Given a common inspiration, three furniture makers create a diversity of designs

BY MARK SCHOFIELD

I'm sure I'm not the only woodworker who has embarked on a project without first working out all the details. After seeing the graceful arches of a bridge spanning Connecticut's Housatonic River, I recently rushed into building an arched-leg table (see photo, below).

I did a quick sketch of the table, built a bending form, and steam-bent some ash arches. The first surprise was how springy the thin arches were; clearly they would need some kind of brace to stop them from widening and the table from getting progressively lower. As I was driving to work, I wondered: How

would Garrett Hack make such a table? How would Jere Osgood tackle this design?

The readers of *Fine Woodworking* often ask for more design articles, but it is a hard subject to pin down. Asking great furniture designers how they develop their ideas is rather like asking Mozart how he came up with a tune—it's not easily described. To solve my own design dilemma and to share with readers how original designs are created, I decided to give three other woodworkers, each with a reputation for original design, a photo of the bridge for inspiration and basic parameters to see what they would create.

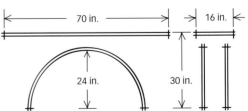

Inspiration and the basic dimensions. The authors designed arched-leg tables based on this concrete bridge in Connecticut. The height, width, and length of the table were specified, as was the height of the arches. Two arches were required to serve as a base.

70 in.   16 in.

24 in.   30 in.

Powerful but poised. The strong stance of the legs contrasts with the thin, floating top and shelf. On the shelf, the undercut edge, the downward sweeping ends of the stretchers, and the space between the shelf and the legs combine to make the panel appear to levitate.

EACH DESIGN BUILDS ON THE LAST ONE

BY WAYNE MARCOUX

When I got *Fine Woodworking's* letter, I thought, "They must be mind readers." I had just visited a gallery where I exhibit and noticed the perfect spot to display a long, narrow sofa or hall table. Not only did the arched-leg table's dimensions fit perfectly, but the design fortuitously built on some of my previous creations.

I started sketching, thinking back to my earlier work: I had built a curved-leg table where the front legs were set closer together than those at the back, with a rectangular top and a half-moon shelf (see top photo, right). The table sold, but the design had an abstract look to it with the top and shelf in conflict. On the next table I tried for a more symmetrical look, with the aprons and stretchers crossing diagonally and a convex shelf complementing the concave edges of the top (see bottom photo, right). This produced a more graceful form that looked correct from any angle.

However, when I saw the idea of having the legs as two complete arches, I knew that was the missing element. I drew up an initial design using tapered laminations for stiffness, but strictly observing the set dimensions. On the final plans, I diverged. The difference between the overall height of the table and the 26-in. outside radius of the arched legs meant having a 3-in. apron. I preferred the more dynamic look of the top supported by the legs, so I lowered the height and had the top rest directly on the crown of the crossing legs. For extra support I added wings that extend 13 in. from the crown along the top of each leg. Viewed in perspective, the form has a very animalistic stance.

The tabletop is 1 in. thick with a 20° bevel cut on the underside while the top is still rectangular. The concave edges are cut through the slope, making the top appear thicker in the center than at the ends. With the long cantilever off the saddle, this gives the top a light and lofty look.

The shelf ends are similar to those of the tabletop, beveled and then profiled, but the sides are profiled and then beveled, making the front edge appear only ¼ in. thick.

Wayne Marcoux is a furniture maker in Manchester, N.H.

Good, better, best. Marcoux's curved-leg table designs have progressed from one where the legs are spaced in pairs (top photo), to one where the legs are aligned but are not complete arcs (lower photo), to the design for this article (top illustration).

BOTH BRIDGES AND TABLES MUST CARRY A LOAD

BY GARRETT
HACK

Given this challenge, my thoughts turned to the couple of covered bridges in our small Vermont town and how their simple, yet very strong, arched trusses work so well after almost 200 years. I also immediately saw the differences between engineering a bridge and a table: The major one is that while a bridge's arches are braced by the banks of the river, the arches on a table will spread when subjected to any downward pressure. One solution is to make the arch heavier, but that would negate some of the design's elegance. A second question is how to make a rigid connection to the tabletop if it joins only the apex of the arch.

My solution for each side of the table was to add half-arches to the full arches, marrying them with vertical posts so that they reinforce each other yet everything remains light in cross section. The half-arches strengthen the single arches, making them less apt to spread under load, and the load on the top is distributed along a number of points. To counteract racking forces across the width of the table, two stretchers spaced well apart connect the vertical posts. In my initial sketch the two posts

Graceful yet grounded. Inspired by the strength, grace, and longevity of his local covered bridges in Vermont, Hack created a radical design where opposing forces keep the table together and support the top.

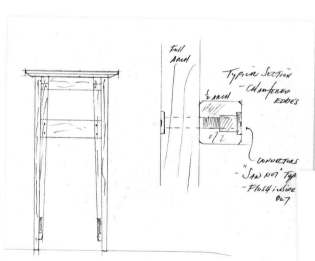

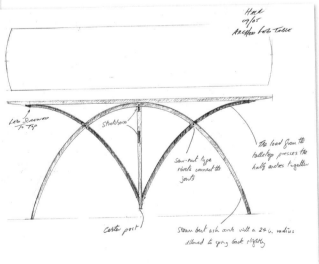

Hack's design uses two arches made from steam-bent ash. To control the springback, a central post and two half-arches are employed on each side of the table. The arches taper from 1 in. by 1 in. at the top to ⅝ in. by ⅝ in. at the foot. The arches, half-arches, and posts are connected with flat-head nuts and bolts, similar to those found on saw handles.

One Editor's Creation

Already committed to steam-bent arches, I couldn't use the laminated designs created by Osgood or Marcoux. I needed to brace the arches, but I also wanted to keep them uncluttered. For this reason I rejected wooden stretchers as too bulky, and opted for steel wire. John White, Fine Woodworking's resourceful shop manager, solved the problem of joinery by passing the wire through threaded brass inserts. The two arches, now resembling bows, were stiff and strong.

Because the steam-bent arches are under tension along their upper surfaces and under compression on the lower edges, I kept the mortises for the crosspieces thin and located them in the center of the arches. A third arch was cut to provide flying supports for the ends of the tabletop.

I gave all four sides of the tabletop a convex curve, and then beveled the underside with a panel-raising bit on a router table. I bleached the whole table using two-part bleach, but when dry-assembled it appeared too monotone, so I dyed the crosspieces and wing supports black.

I mostly build period furniture, and once in a while it's liberating to put aside the past and improvise.
—Mark Schofield

touched the floor, giving the table six feet, but in my final design the post is cut back slightly so that the table rests solely on the four points of the main arches.

Steam-bending is my method of choice to form the arches, using a single elliptical form. Minor variations in the arches using this method would not be noticeable. I would use ash, which bends extremely well into smooth curves. The wood should be cut to nearly its final dimension, then planed and steam-bent. After a few days of drying, the parts will be ready for joinery.

The joinery follows the bridge analogy: Simple flat-head nuts and bolts connect the main arches to the half-arches and each post and allow some flexing, yet don't diminish the strength of any member as mortises might. The absence of glue would allow the table to be leveled on its four feet before the bolts are snugged up.

Garrett Hack is a contributing editor to Fine Woodworking *magazine.*

High-tension table. On Schofield's table, the arches are held in shape by picture-frame wire strung across the base.

DON'T LET CONSTRUCTION WORRIES CONSTRAIN YOUR DESIGNS

BY JERE OSGOOD

I wasn't surprised when the proposal arrived with its single photograph. It is one of the ways I work. I try to stay alert to interesting forms and to note them in my sketchbook. Great forms can and should be carried over to furniture; in this case I was inspired by the bridge's arches.

Generally I work out the engineering and joinery after a design is under way: I feel we should design first and then find the techniques to carry it out. Despite its simple appearance, this table involves fairly advanced woodworking from the tapered lamination arches to the angled stub tenons. I believe it is worth the effort; many pieces wouldn't be made if we had to stick to easy, straightforward joinery.

I used tapered laminations for the arches because they create a stiffer arch, less liable to spread under load. The

outer legs are needed only to support the ends of the tabletop. They could be made from solid wood, but I would laminate them to harmonize with the arches. I designed the two arches to lean inward by 2° each. If they were vertical, at first glance they would appear to be splayed outward at the top. It is subtle, but I've seen tables designed both ways, and the more complicated joinery with the inward-leaning arches and legs is worth the effort.

I always do a full-size drawing; it helps me discover and tackle difficult areas such as the joint between the middle beams and the arches. Even though this table has no traditional apron, I kept the top of the end legs straight for about 4 in. to emphasize the introduction of the taper.

Jere Osgood is a member of the New Hampshire Furniture Masters Association.

Simple and subtle. The base of Osgood's table consists of a pair of elliptical, laminated arches that lean inward by 2° to avoid the optical illusion of leaning outward. The tabletop is chamfered on the top and tapers slightly at each end. It is supported in the center by a pair of beams, through-tenoned into the arches, and at the ends by four outer legs that also are laminated and lean inward with the arches.

Full-size drawings simplify complicated joints. Because the arched legs lean inward by 2°, the stub tenons of the middle beams must be angled the same amount.

CONTRIBUTOR INDEX

Roger Heitzman
750 Whispering Pines
Scotts Valley, CA 95066
(831) 438-1118 (studio)
(831) 345-5411 (cell)
roger@heitzmanstudios.com
www.heitzmanstudios.com

David Hogan
19062 Alamo Lane
Yorba Linda, CA 92886
dhogan@fullcoll.edu

Steve Holman
Holman Studios
Fine Custom Furniture
P.O.Box 572
Dorset, VT 05251
Tel: (802) 867-0131
Fax: (802) 867-0255
www.holmanstudios.com

Hank Holzer
2118 E. Olive Street
Seattle,WA 98122
(206) 324-8538
holzerames@aol.com
www.nwfinewoodworking.com/hank_holzer/index

James Hoyne
P.O.Box 161184
Big Sky, MT 59716
(406) 995-2726
www.highaltitudewoodworking.com

Katie Hudnall
905 Roseneath Road
Richmond, VA 23221
(804) 387-2932
Katiehudnall@hotmail.com
www.katiehudnall.com

David Hurwitz
David Hurwitz Originals
23 Randolph Ave.
Randolph, VT 05060
(802) 728-9399
dho@davidhurwitzoriginals.com
www.davidhurwitzoriginals.com

Bill Huston
Huston and Company
Designers and Builders of Fine Custom Furniture
Kennebunkport, ME 04046
(207) 967-2345
bill@hustonandcompany.com
www.hustonandcompany.com

Matt Hutton
24 Mayfield Street
Portland, ME 04103
(207) 749-4731
mhutton@meca.edu
www.studio24b.com

Craig Jentz
5217 Logan Avenue South
Minneapolis, MN 55419
cjjentz@q.com

Clark Kellogg
2303-B Dunlavy
Houston, TX 77006
info@kelloggfurniture.com
www.kelloggfurniture.com

Tony Kenway
496 Coorabell Road
Coorabell, NSW 2479
Australia
+61 2 66 847102
Kenway5@bigpond.com
www.tonykenwayfurniture.com

Aspy Khambatta
1433 Everett Street
El Cerrito, CA 96530
(510) 604-7288
aspy-judy@comcast.net

Scott M. King
Meadowview, Mayfield Road
Mayfield, St. George, BB19045
Barbados
(246) 234-1512
scott@scottkingfurniture.com
www.scottkingfurniture.com

Greg Klassen
Box 415
Lynden, WA 98264
(360) 305-5070
www.gregklassen.com

Robert Kopf
1115 Dodson Ridge Road
Walnut Cove, NC 27052
(336) 591-4973
bobkopf@msn.com

Mark Levin
P.O.Box 109
San Jose, NM 87565-0109
(575) 421-3207
markslevin@yahoo.com
www.marklevin.com

Peter Loh
10439 SE 14th Street
Bellevue, WA 98004
(206) 696-1130
contact@peterloh.com
www.peterloh.com

John Marckworth
535 Cass St.
Port Townsend, WA 98368
john@marckworthdesign.com
www.marckworthdesign.com

Loy Martin
150 Grant Avenue, #F
Palo Alto, CA 94306
(650) 325-3416
loym@batnet.com

Ryan McNew
6701 N. College Ave. #412
Indianapolis, IN 46220
(912) 655-4459
ryan@ryanmcnewfurniture.com
www.ryanmcnewfurniture.com

Jeff Miller
J. Miller Handcrafted Furniture
1774 W. Lunt Avenue
Chicago, IL 60626
(773) 761-3311
info@furnituremaking.com
www.furnituremaking.com

Curt Minier
curtminier@gmail.com

Thomas J. Monahan
314 21st St. NW
Cedar Rapids, IA 52405
(319) 365-6482 (home)
(319) 560-7929 (cell)
thomasjmonahan@imonmail.com
www.thomasjmonahan.com

Hugh Montgomery
14645 Sunrise Drive, NE
Bainbridge Island, WA 98110
(360) 779-8300
info@hughmontgomery.com
www.hughmontgomery.com

Pat Morrow
420 Snyder Mountain Road
Evergreen, CO 80439
(303) 674-1203
pat@trailmixstudio.com
www.trailmixstudio.com

S. Lloyd Natof
1217 W. Monroe
Chicago, IL 60607
(312) 733-4205
Lloyd@SLNATOF.com
www.SLNATOF.com

Jeff O'Brien
18740 Nixon Avenue
West Linn, OR 97068
(503) 639-8758
jeff@dogwood-design.com
www.dogwood-design.com

Todd Ouwehand
12014 Mitchell Ave.
Los Angeles, CA 90066
(310) 903-9257
toddman57@aol.com
www.toddouwehand.com

Todd Partridge
P.O. Box 7101
San Diego, CA 92167
todd@toddpartridgedesign.com
www.toddpartridgedesign.com

Alexandria Reznikoff
(973) 715-7355
woodbyalex@gmail.com
www.woodbyalex.com

Kevin Rodel
14 Maine Street, Box 63
Brunswick, ME 04011
(207) 725-7252
Kevin@kevinrodel.com
www.kevinrodel.com

Gary Rogowski
The Northwest Woodworking Studio
A School for Woodworking
1002 SE 8th Ave
Portland, OR 97214
(503) 284-1644
www.northwestwoodworking.com

Seth Rolland
Custom Furniture Design
1039 Jackson Street
Port Townsend, WA 98368
(360) 379-0414
Seth@olypen.com
www.sethrolland.com

Jim Postell
161 Lafayette Circle
Cincinnati, OH 45220
(513) 861-9136
Jim.postell@uc.edu
www.daap.uc.edu/people/profiles/posteljc

Roger Savatteri
532 Van Velsir Drive
Monte Nido, CA 91302
(310) 625-2887
savatteridesigns@earthlink.net
www.savatteridesigns.com

Jason Schneider
P.O.Box 5598
Snowmass Village, CO 81615
Schneiderj2000@yahoo.com
www.jasonschneiderfurniture.com

James Schriber
P.O.Box 1145
New Milford, CT 06776
(860) 354-6452
js@jamesschriber.com
www.jamesschriber.com

Thomas R. Schrunk
3108 32nd Ave NE
Minneapolis, MN 55418
tschrunk@aol.com
www.thomasschrunk.com

Kay Selle
325 Beechwood Lane
Coppell, TX 75019
(972) 462-8023
kay@selledesign.com
www.selledesign.com

Mark Sfirri
1669 Pineville Road
New Hope, PA 18938
(215) 794-8125
marksfirri@gmail.com

Jon Siegel
Big Tree Turnings
258 Breezy Hill Road
Wilmot, NH 03287-4111
(603) 768-5882
big@proctornet.com
www.bigtreeturnings.com
www.bigtreetools.com

Michael Singer Fine Woodworking
1170 El Solyo Heights Drive
Felton, CA 95018
(831) 335-3167
mms@msfinewoodworking.com
www.msfinewoodworking.com

Greg Smith
947 Cedar Street
Fort Bragg, CA 95437
(707) 962-0838
GSmith@prxy.com
www.gregbsmith.com

Christopher Solar
www.christophersolar.com

Paul Stefanski
www.paulstefanski.com

Craig Thibodeau
6036 Arosa Street
San Diego, CA 92115
(619) 981-4508
info@ctfinefurniture.com
www.ctfinefurniture.com

John Thoe
2201 NE 120th Street
Seattle, WA 98125
(206) 505-6229
www.johnthoe.com

Peter Thompson
151 Walton Mill Road
Cornville, ME 04976
(207) 474-6182
peter@peterthompsonfurniture.com
www.peterthompsonfurniture.com

Katrina Tompkins
www.katrinatompkins.com

Peter Turner
126 Boothby Ave.
S. Portland, ME 04106
(207) 799-5503
Petersturner@hotmail.com
www.petersturner.com

David Upfill-Brown
Center for Furniture Craftsmanship
25 Mill Street
Rockport, ME 04856
upfillbrown@hotmail.com

J-P Vilkman
Stuurenkatu 26 B 33
Fin-00510 Helsinki
Finland
+358 40 740 2031
j-p@j-pvilkman.com
www.j-pvilkman.com

Paulus Wanrooij
708 Harpswell Neck Road
Harpswell, ME 04079
(207) 833-5026
paulus@paulusfurniture.com
www.paulusfurniture.com

Kimberly Winkle
1862 Puckett Point Road
Smithville, TN 37166
(615) 597-5138
wimkinkle@yahoo.com

Leah Woods
55 Summer Street #4
Dover, NH 03820
Leah.woods@unh.edu
www.leahwoodsstudio.com

Susan Working
PO Box 5986
Snowmass Village, CO 81615
(970) 923-3181, Ext. 234
sworking@andersonranch.org

CREDITS